DESKTOP PUBLISHING
A Complete Course

GW00633745

DESKTOP PUBLISHING

A COMPLETE COURSE

DAWN MULHOLLAND

GILL & MACMILLAN

GILL & MACMILLAN LTD

GOLDENBRIDGE

DUBLIN 8

WITH ASSOCIATED COMPANIES THROUGHOUT THE WORLD

© DAWN MULHOLLAND 1996

0 7171 2362 6

PRINT ORIGINATION IN IRELAND BY DESIGN IMAGE

CONTENTS

ACKNOWLEDGMENTS

To all users of desktop publishing applications, teachers and students, and especially those who unknowingly follow in the footsteps of Gutenberg.

I would like to thank all those students who tested the exercises and those who generously created images and logos. I had specialist help from a colleague, Paul Whelan, at various stages of the book's development, for which I am particularly grateful.

Thank you to the editorial team at Gill & Macmillan who frequently offered professional guidance. I am indebted, also, to the anonymous reviewers whose critical comments were especially valuable.

Every author's family makes a major contribution to a book and so grateful thanks go to them for their prolonged support.

For permission to reproduce illustrations, grateful acknowledgment is made to the following:
H D Design; Bloomsbury Books (for illustrations taken from *The Illustrated Dictionary of Science and Technology*); Ward Lock; Masterclip Graphics, Inc. (Clipart Copyright © 1996 Masterclip Graphics, Inc.) and GST Technology Ltd; Woodstock Realisations.

INTRODUCTION

This book has been written because teachers have no general guidelines to follow to ensure that their students will achieve good results in examinations up to Level II in all major examinations, including NCVA, City and Guilds, Royal Society of Arts and Pitman. **Desktop publishing** can be a difficult subject to teach unless there are plenty of examples to teach from with specifications provided.

The exercises in this book take students from an absolutely empty screen to levels beyond the present examination requirements. Unfortunately, the examination bodies have left out the creative dimension that desktop publishing offers, and almost all the examinations require very traditional output, in some cases asking for unsuitable typographical features like underlining of subheadings and requiring a rigid layout in relation to alignment and point size. This is particularly true of Level I assignments. I have retained these requirements, with reservations, in some examples, but dropped them in subsequent exercises.

It must be emphasised that this book contains *exercises*, which by their nature are abstractions from reality. On the other hand, many of the exercises are taken from the type of material that arrives in any household.

Of course, it is correct that the essential foundations be examined. However, there is plenty more that students can do, and I have seen many in class who revel in the release from the straitjacket of other computer applications. We have in desktop publishing an opportunity to expand a pupil's experience of computing, while satisfying their need to be inventive and stamp individuality on their output. I feel these examples and exercises will do that.

This is a complete course designed to suit the general principles of all the most widely-used packages, mainly on IBM compatible machines. However, as a Mac user myself, I know there is now such an overlap that there should be little difficulty for teachers in making the slight keyboard or menu changes necessary for Mac users.

There are about one hundred exercises designed to be used in the course of a year of two class sessions per week. Enthusiastic students will complete all of them and be able to tackle the assignments at the very end of the book. Teachers should be flexible in some of the exercises in Part Three where students have ideas of their own, and Part Four may become just a springboard for the able student. Students can be referred to the *Good work practices* section and to the section on *Principles of good design*, to check that their ideas still fall within the bounds of acceptability.

The divisions in the book represent the stages through which most courses go.

Part One	Learning the essentials
Part Two	Expanding on these fundamentals
Part Three	Preparing for Level 1 and 2 for all prestigious examining bodies
Part Four	Showing proficiency and creativeness in the discipline and becoming ready for employment

Desktop publishing should be a most enjoyable subject to teach and learn, giving early satisfying results. The complete package in this book of exercises, with accompanying text and images on disk, should make that possible.

WHAT IS DESKTOP PUBLISHING?

Desktop publishing is a term used to describe the computerised production of multiple copies of documents, leaflets, notices, advertisements, brochures and books. Many of the terms used in the preparation of these documents have come straight from the world of printing, while others are from the computer sphere.

There are many applications of this skill in our daily lives. The majority of the newspapers we read, as well as books and magazines, are prepared using a desktop publishing package. In these instances, the page by page output is made into **camera-ready material** and then, via a metal sheet containing the full page image, the publication is sent to press. This means that multiple copies, millions in the case of newspapers and magazines, are produced in a single run.

Another application of this process is for individuals, either within a company or working from a client brief, to prepare documents for circulation to a more specific target audience. This may be to other employees or groups within the company and subsidiaries, or to the public in the case of flyers and other advertisements. In these instances, the number of units in the run is likely to be much lower than in the case of newspapers.

In whatever field desktop publishing is used, the principles are the same and are inherited directly from the world of printing. These principles in turn are handed down from the original diversifiers of knowledge and wisdom — the monks (scribes) who painstakingly copied manuscripts so that the mysteries of the written word could be shared by more people. They brought structure, colour, consistency, variety and images to the page, just as we expect to find these elements in our daily reading.

A desktop publishing package is unusual in its nature in that it manipulates items produced in other packages and arranges them into a preconstructed shape. Usually, the best results are obtained by using the package's manipulative features rather than its drawing and text-creating elements. When these are needed in any quantity, or to an extremely high quality, it is best to construct them in packages specifically designed for that purpose.

We can see from the diagram on page 4 that the central process is indeed desktop publishing, but, for it to function most effectively, **word processing,** as well as **drawing** and **design** packages, should be used, in conjunction with **scanners**, and so leave the desktop publishing package to combine all these elements into a functional whole.

The desktop publishing package provides the *structure* to combine the elements effectively. We should be aware of what to expect from an efficient desktop publishing package:

a. The ability to place text and illustrations with accuracy on a page design that aids the reader in absorbing the contents. The package must be able to respond to design briefs to give flexible presentation and yet maintain consistency. This is achieved by providing for 'once-off' publications and also for the item that is to be published regularly.

b. We expect the desktop publishing package to import text and make it appealing by presenting it in a variety of fonts.

c. The illustrative part of the document, either photographs which have been scanned or graphic items designed in a specific package, should be handled by the desktop publishing process in much the same way. It should be able to scale the image to the required size, crop unnecessary parts and place the finished product very precisely. The desktop publishing package itself will provide the drawn lines, colour, tints and embellishments to enhance the overall look and readability.

You will see from the diagram how a variety of software packages work together to produce what we call desktop publishing.

The basic **hardware** requirements are:

CPU (central processing unit)

Monitor (screen)

Input devices (keyboard, mouse)

Output device (printer)

A scanner is optional at present, either handheld or flatbed.

Support systems for a desktop publishing package

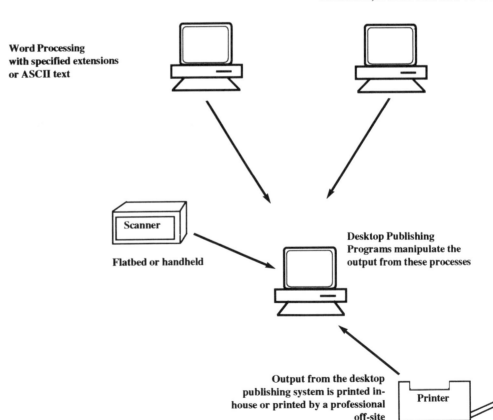

Design Work
Photographs, scanned images
Paint programs from Adobe Illustrator,
Adobe Photoshop, Freelance Graphics,
Corel Draw, or retrieval from a CD ROM

Word Processing
with specified extensions
or ASCII text

Scanner

Flatbed or handheld

Desktop Publishing
Programs manipulate the
output from these processes

Output from the desktop
publishing system is printed in-
house or printed by a professional
off-site

Printer

TYPOGRAPHY

Any study of desktop publishing must include an appreciation of typography. This area is concerned with the way text is presented in terms of typeface, type size and the space surrounding each character. We know already that reading material is made up of words (some of which are in capitals), figures and punctuation. These alphanumeric units are the tools of the desktop publisher's trade. A small change in size or **leading** can have an enormous effect on a piece of textual matter.

There are essentially two typefaces — serif and sans serif. The **serif** is the most often encountered, as it is used in almost all areas of communication. It is also the typeface that makes reading easier and is, therefore, used in novels, magazines and newspapers, as well as shorter documents. Its identifying feature is that the characters have small 'feet' at the beginning and end of each stroke.

The **sans serif** typeface has no extensions to its strokes, *sans* meaning without, in French. It has a simple, modern appearance and is widely used in short pieces, subheadings and some headlines. It is also becoming more widely used for body copy in magazines and manuals and is used as the body text in this book.

Characters

The use of the word **font** should be restricted to the description of a group of alphanumeric and punctuation characters all having the same features. For example, the Times Roman font describes all the sizes and thicknesses of all the characters, figures and punctuation marks of a particular serif typeface. The Palatino font describes a serif typeface which has different widths in its strokes from other fonts in the serif category. In Appendix Three you will see the two typefaces and several examples of fonts which fit under these headings.

The **x-height** is an important feature of all fonts. It measures the size of those characters or parts of a character which rest on the baseline but neither go above or below the height of an **x**. Thus, **a, o, r, v**, etc., as well as the bowl of **b** and **d**, represent the x-height.

Other important terms are **ascender** and **descender**. The first describes that part of a character which rises above the x-height (**h, b** and **k** are examples), while a descender is that part of a character which reaches beneath the x-height (**g**, **y**, **p** and **j** are examples of this).

One other feature you should identify is the **ligature**. This is a feature of some fonts where certain combinations of letters lend themselves to being joined. It is the join which is the ligature. Some examples are

fi fl ff ffi ffl

TYPE STYLES

There are several type styles in general use and examples are shown here.

Sentences	(normal)
Sentences	(bold)
Sentences	(italic)
Sentences	(bold italic)
5° degrees	(superior or superscript)
H_2O	(subscript or inferior character)

Measurements in desktop publishing have descended from the printing industries of France and England, with some reference to the American system as well. Nearly all packages, reference books and manuals refer to areas of space, margins, indents, etc., in millimetres, and I have maintained that convention in the course.

However, the size of characters is almost universally referred to in point sizes. A point is approximately $\frac{1}{72}$ of an inch, and that rounded figure is an accepted measurement. The point system describes the height of the font from baseline to the top of the capitals. However, there is a small space within this measurement to prevent decenders meeting the top of the capitals.

One inch	**Text**	72 points
Half an inch	**Text**	36 points
Quarter of a inch	**Text**	18 points

A point size of 72 is therefore one inch, 36 pts (the accepted abbreviation) is half an inch and 18 pts a quarter of an inch, and so on. There is, of course, a huge range between, above and below these, but those mentioned here give you something to relate to. You should remember that one font of, say, 24 pts is likely to be different from another of the same point size because of its design. You can observe this in the sample fonts in Appendix Three.

One other measurement you might meet is the **em**. This is a *linear* unit of measurement in which the square of the typesize is indicated. Today it is used mostly to indicate the amount a paragraph is indented when not using millimetres. There is an **en** measurement as well, which is half an em.

Leading (pronounced *ledding*) is the term which describes the space between each line. It is approximately one fifth more than the type size. It is written as part of the type size description: 12 on 14 pt leading (or 30 on 36 pt leading), which means 12 pt type set with 14 pts of leading.

THE MOUSE

The **mouse** is a pointing device used to manipulate objects within a document. It is a handheld device which has a magnetic ball underneath it that relays data back to the screen about its position on a surface in relation to the screen layout.

USING THE MOUSE

The following terms explain the techniques for using the mouse.

Click	Press the left button and immediately release it without moving the mouse.
Right click	Press and release the right mouse button without moving the mouse.
Double click	Press and release the left button twice in quick succession without moving the mouse.
Press and hold	Press the left button and hold it down. (This is necessary at times for the computer to accumulate the data being selected.)
Drag	Press the left button and hold it down as the mouse is moved. The move is completed when you release the button.

Users of the Apple Mac will have just one button on the mouse to hold down while selecting options.

PRINCIPLES OF GOOD DESIGN

Desktop publishing is most successful when the principles of good design are applied. Being able to use the package proficiently is not enough. There are underlying rules which, when observed, turn an ordinary document into one with character and style.

Character and style are qualities which apply to simplicity and effectiveness. The following points will help you to create publications which bear the hallmarks of good design.

The **audience** for whom the publication is intended has to be established. This information will dictate the overall look — small or large print, formal or relaxed typographical impact, the quantity of, and emphasis placed on, illustrative material, whether colour is used, together with the density and amount of text.

The **objective** of the document is the next important factor to establish. If it is simply to inform an interested target audience of straight facts, the design features will be different from a document aimed at an audience which needs to be attracted and kept interested in a topic which it would easily pass over.

The **structure** of the document can now be considered, which will help to bring consistency as well as diversity and interest to it.

The **four elements** of most publications are **text**, **illustrations**, **graphics** (using the drawing tools) and **white space**.

The most acceptable **ratio of white space** to the total page area is about half and half. The minimum requirement is one third of white space to two thirds text and other features.

Body text is nearly always in a small serif font and, if dense, should be broken up with paragraphs, 'pull quotes' and subheadings in larger and bolder typefaces.

The **reading line length** should be kept to 7 to 10 words (34 – 40 characters) and generous leading should be set wherever possible. Unjustified alignment also helps readers, as the eye is pre-warned of a line end and can take up the new line more easily.

Plan out your communication before you start work on the computer and remember that, in the West, we read from top left to bottom right and this principle should determine the layout of the page.

Typeface changes should be kept to a minimum (2 – 3 maximum) and be consistent in their use.

Fancy fonts should be used sparingly — use them for special effects only. Never use an enhancement unnecessarily — white space speaks equally loudly.

Consistency in the layout of multi-page documents is vital with regard to column widths, gutters, margins, as well as having variety from one page to another in the use of images and graphics.

A **style sheet** (**template** or **master page**) that is part of the desktop publishing package is the way to determine all these items and make the layout task easy. Double pages must be considered as a whole, not as individual pages, as the overall balance and look of the spread is important.

Text and illustrations should be integrated as closely as possible. This means that the style of the image and its contents should reflect the subject and its style, as well as being of a pleasing size in relation to the total page — neither too large nor too small.

Bottom **margin** measurements should be a little deeper than those for the top. Even margins are seen by the reader as smaller at the bottom and the document appears to be very close to the edge of the page.

Colour should be used very sparingly, to add interest to typography or to draw the reader's attention to images, graphics or logos, but in the main frugality is the key to success with colour.

A **preliminary sketch** should be worked out on the guidelines given here, so that you sit down at the computer with a clear indication of your ideas, although these may change and develop during the document's creation.

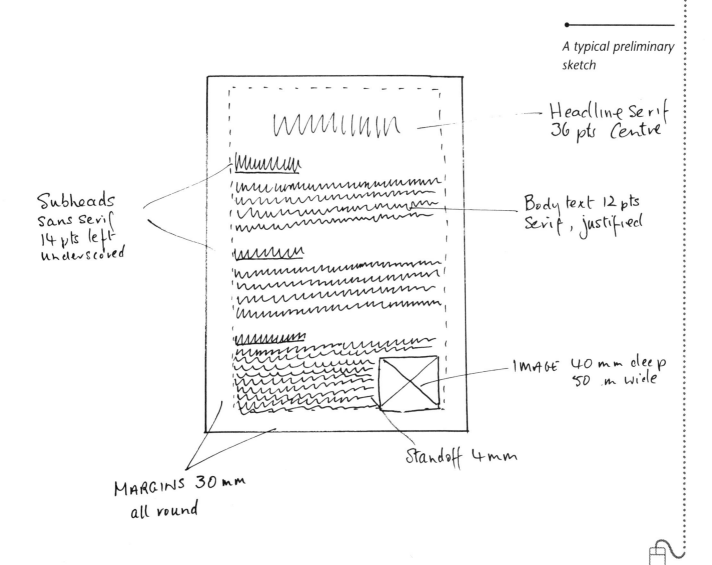

A typical preliminary sketch

Headline Serif 36 pts Centre

Subheads sans serif 14 pts left underscored

Body text 12 pts Serif, justified

IMAGE 40 mm deep 50 m wide

Standoff 4mm

MARGINS 30 mm all round

THE OPENING SCREEN AND PAPER ORIENTATION

Below are two typical **opening screens** and you will see how similar they are. Your package will have either identical properties or features that perform exactly the same functions. The exercises that follow require you to be familiar with the opening screen of your program and to be able to use the mouse. (See page 7 for mouse use.)

You will notice that your screen provides you with an 'electronic' page, which is the printing area surrounded by a pasteboard on which you can store parts of a document as you create them and then assemble them on the page. You will also notice that the dimensions of the page represent an A4 sheet with the narrowest side at the top. This is called **portrait** orientation and this is how every package defaults on startup. You can change the defaults if your work is mostly in **landscape,** where the longest side is at the top, or change the orientation in Page Setup (File menu) for those occasions when landscape is required.

PORTRAIT

LANDSCAPE

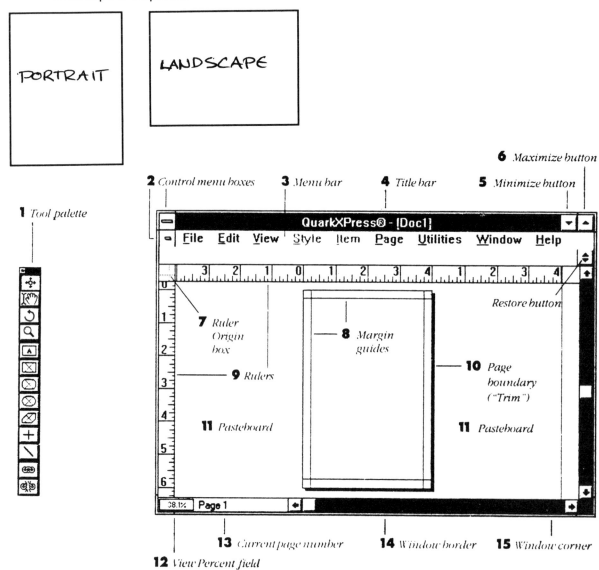

1 *Tool palette*

2 *Control menu boxes* **3** *Menu bar* **4** *Title bar* **5** *Minimize button* **6** *Maximize button*

QuarkXPress® - [Doc1]

File **Edit** **View** **Style** **Item** **Page** **Utilities** **Window** **Help**

Restore button

7 *Ruler Origin box*

8 *Margin guides*

9 *Rulers*

10 *Page boundary ("Trim")*

11 *Pasteboard*

11 *Pasteboard*

38.1% Page 1

12 *View Percent field*

13 *Current page number* **14** *Window border* **15** *Window corner*

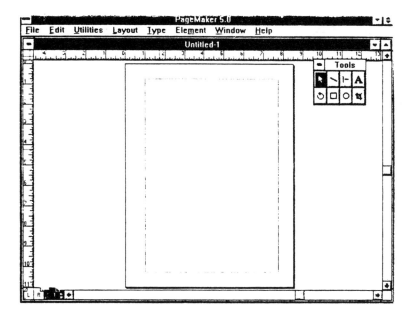

*Choices from the
page setup
dialog box*

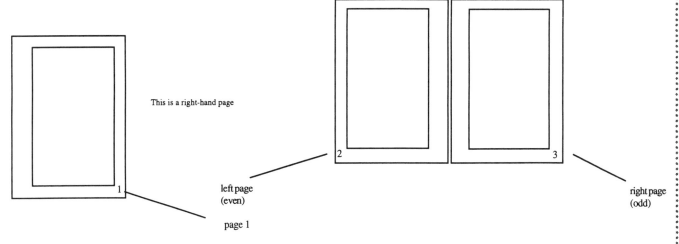

This is a right-hand page

left page
(even)

right page
(odd)

page 1

The diagram above shows a single page or page 1. A double-sided document would have printed matter on the reverse.

The diagram above shows a double-page spread. Here the right page is a mirror image of the left. Often a wider inner margin is required so that pages can be bound either in a folder or into a book, booklet or signature. You can alter the setting to even margins at Page Setup in the margins box or change the default so that your choice of settings appears every time you start with a new document.

GOOD WORK PRACTICES

All computer users should observe several simple rules to ensure that they get the benefit of speed and efficiency from their equipment. Keeping to the following recommendations will save you many occasions of stress and annoyance.

1 Create a **directory,** or directories, for your files on the hard drive. If you expect to save onto floppies, create directories on these disks too.

2 **Save** often.

3 Save with a **file name** that helps you to recognise the contents. If your package has a summary option, use it to define the file contents.

4 Be prepared to **correct from draft output** from DTP several times if necessary. It is at print time that inaccuracies in placement and text become obvious.

5 Get someone else to **proofread** your document and ask them to give an opinion on the overall 'look' of it.

6 Save all relevant files to do with a document with filenames that relate them to each other. You might have **word processing**, **art work**, **charts**, **images** and **scanned elements** to store for one printout.

7 Turn off the images detail to **Grey Out**, so that you can move about the screen quickly.

8 As you become proficient in any package, learn the **keyboard shortcuts**. This, together with the last point, greatly speeds up the creation of page layouts.

9 **Spell check** all your word processing in that package. Then you have the accurate text stored for all future use.

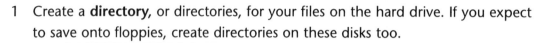
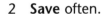
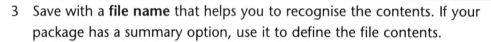
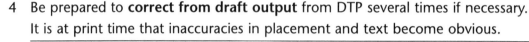
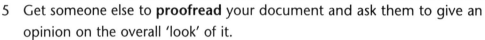
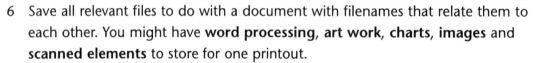

NOTES TO TEACHERS

SAVING FILES

Some students come to desktop publishing without any previous knowledge of computing and meet problems associated more with computers than their ability to use the program. A basic skill for students is to be able to save a file in the correct directory and retrieve it again. Many teachers will confirm how difficult this can be and below I have set out a five-point routine for students to follow to explain the steps on IBM compatible machines. Before using it, however, it would be vital to set up directories for your class, and as far as possible students should keep to the same work station. The directories could be created for a class or course title and have one for completed publications and one each for texts and images. (You may also wish to use subdirectories from the start, though I find students have plenty to deal with getting files into directories!) Then, as the course develops, students will be importing elements according to examination requirements and as they would in a work situation.

If you are running under Windows and have not set up directories before, then in Program Manager's Main window choose **File Manager**. Ensuring you have the C drive highlighted, from the File menu select **Create Directory**. In the ensuing dialog box, type

PUBLISH

and press **OK**. Again, with the C drive highlighted, select **Create Directory** and type

DTPTEXTS

in the dialog box. Repeat these steps to create a directory for

IMAGES

You now have three related directories on the C drive in which to place your files during production. You may need to add to these for examination purposes and I would advise you to back up all your work for exams on the A drive as you do them, rather than at the end of each assignment.

To avoid saving your work directly onto the hard drive, use the directories you have created to **Save**, using the following routine after loading the package.

1	From the File menu select **New**
2	Accept with **OK** the defaults on the Page Setup dialog box, or insert the required margins (check the correct orientation is selected, A4 portrait for the first ten exercises)
3	Input your text and other elements
4	From File menu select **Save As**

    a. Select the correct **Drive** (C if using the above guide or A if saving to floppies)

    b. Select the correct **Directory** (Publish)

    c. Type in an eight-character name (suggested in all exercises)

    d. Select **OK** or **Enter**

5 From File menu select **Close**

RECALLING A FILE

1 From the File menu select **Open**

2 a. From the dialog box select the **Drive** (C in these guidelines or A if recalling from a floppy)

    b. Select the **Directory** (Publish)

    c. Select with a double click the file name you gave the publication on saving

    d. Click on **OK** or press **Enter**

The file you last worked on appears on the screen for further editing. You need only **Save** now, as once a file is saved with a name it will retain that identifying label.

You may wish your students to **Save As** immediately they open a file (though I prefer to leave this concept until a little later), in which case the same routine as above can be followed, postponing the document assembly until after **Save As**.

USING THE DISK THAT COMES WITH THIS BOOK

By installing this disk using the following instructions, two subdirectories (or folders) will be created on your hard disk: image.96 and text.96.

Insert the disk into drive A

1 Installing at the DOS prompt

    Log on to the A drive by typing A: and press the **Enter** key

    Type INSTALL and press the **Enter** key.

2 Installing under Windows

    (i) Windows 3.0 or higher

        Under File in the Program Manager select **Run** and type

        A:INSTALL and click on **OK**

    (ii) Windows 95

        From the task bar select **Run** and type

        A:INSTALL

These directories or folders will contain the material students need to complete the exercises as they appear in the book. Students' completed documents and any text they create or images they scan or create in paint and draw programs can be saved to the directories made earlier.

All the texts for the longer exercises are provided and almost every image is on the disk — some in colour. The texts can be used in sections for any practice work or mock-ups and to practise copy fitting in any preliminary work they might do.

Teachers should note that most packages can easily have their defaults overridden by, for example, changing the margins in the Page Setup dialog box without having a document on screen. All subsequent documents will then appear with these settings. The margin defaults for the first eight exercises can be set at 25 mm all round so that students need not make any reference to these until exercise 9, when they will have developed some expertise.

By following the specifications in this book, students will produce attractive material that originated on mostly A4, some on A5 and a few on A3. Every exercise is illustrated with the finished product, but for technical reasons it is not possible to reproduce many of them in their original size. Students will quickly learn from their own output the relative sizes of type and white space and use the illustrations as a guide to the overall appearance of their work. The thumbnails are a quick source of layout instructions and specifications. In the later exercises students can provide their own, practising for the requirements of some examination bodies.

· PART ONE ·

BASIC TECHNIQUES

Before you begin...

...many of these exercises have features that can be previewed in Facts, Examples and Exercises *(page 54).*

▼ EXERCISE 1

CREATING AND SAVING A DOCUMENT

In this exercise you will

1 **enter text**

2 **create text styles**

3 **highlight text and select styles**

4 **move text blocks around the page**

5 **save a file**

6 **print a file**

Set up a **Single Right Page**, portrait orientation, with margins of 25 mm all round. Your desktop publishing package is likely to default to this setup, so accept the defaults by choosing **New** from the File menu.

Using the **text tool**, click within the margins.

Text tool

Change to **Actual Size** in the Page menu so that you can see the top left of the page as set out by your package.

Type the following text when the I-beam appears.

DIRECTORS' MEETING

Room 37 — 2 p m

Chaired by Thelma Klein

Remember to press **Enter** after each line.

This text will appear in the default text, usually 12 pt Roman and left aligned in the top left of the page area. Check for accuracy of text.

Using the text tool, **highlight** the first line (by dragging the pointer across the words with the left mouse button down).

Create the following text specification from the Type or Paragraph menu.

Name   Main
Size   36 pts
Font   Times Roman
Alignment   Centre

In all cases, select the nearest available on your software.

When all these choices have been made, select **OK.** Select **Main** from the Type Style list and observe the change in the text size and position.

Using the text tool, **highlight** line 2.

Create the following text specification from the Type or Paragraph menu.

Name   Place
Size   24 pts
Font   Times Roman
Alignment   Centre

Select **Place** from the Type Style list and observe the change.

Using the text tool, **highlight** line 3.

Click on **Main** in the text specification list, so that this line has the same characteristics as line 1. All three lines are now centred.

This notice needs to be placed centrally down the page, so, using the text tool, click at the first character on the first line and press **Enter** 4 times.

Engage full page view to check for overall look. Adjust the vertical placement, if necessary, as follows: make sure the Number Lock is off (on the keypad at the right of the keyboard), place the text tool just before the first character of the first line and click, press **Enter** to increase the white space at the top or press **Backspace** to reduce the space by one line each time you press this key.

Remember to save your files regularly and, if you have not done so already, **Save As** Dirnot1.??? (using the correct extension) in the drive and directory.

If your tutor has the printer ready, you could print this document by selecting **Print** from the File menu and **1** copy from the Copies box and selecting **OK.**

Scrutinise your finished document for any improvements you could make in layout or choice of font or text size.

DIRECTORS' MEETING
Room 37 - 2pm
Chaired by Thelma Klein

▼ Exercise 2

Recalling, Editing and Saving as a New Name

In this exercise you will

1 **recall a file**

2 **add text**

3 **adjust position of text**

Call up Dirnot1.??? by clicking on **Open** in the File menu, choosing the correct drive and directory if not immediately shown, and click twice on the file name.

Place the text tool after the n of 'Klein' and press **Enter**.

Select **Body Text** from the Text Style palette/list.

Type line 4

Leading Market Research Officer

Type line 5

Video Show at 3.30 pm in Theatre

Highlight the new line 4 and select **Place** from the Type Style list.

*Thumbnail
Exercise 2*

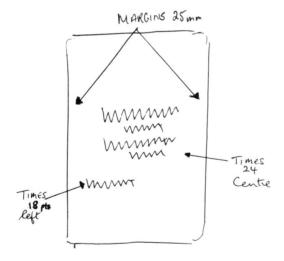

Use the cursor and **Enter** three blank lines.

Highlight line 5.

Create the following text specification from the Type or Paragraph menu.

Name	Vid
Size	18 pts
Font	Times Roman
Alignment	Left

You may have to scroll down the Type Specification list to find Vid — select it and see that the text enlarges.

Confirm the accuracy of the text and correct if necessary. Adjust the vertical placement of the edited announcement. **Save As** for a new document (Dirnot2.???) or over the original with **Save**, according to your tutor's instructions. Choose **Print** from the File menu to print now.

DIRECTORS' MEETING
Room 37 - 2pm
Chaired by Thelma Klein
Leading Market Research Officer

Video Show at 3.30 pm in Theatre

▼ Exercise 3
Graphic Addition and Editing

In this exercise you will

1	**recall a file**
2	**delete text and add text**
3	**add a graphic feature (a frame)**
4	**adjust position of two elements (frame and text)**

Recall Dirnot2.??? from File and **Open**. You will find the file in the directory you used to save the file. Select the drive, the directory and then the correct file extension. You will see the file in an area from which you can select it by clicking on it twice.

Using the **text tool**, move to the figure '7' (line 2) and click.

Backspace two characters and then type

14

Repeat this process for the name in line three, typing in

Martin Hussey

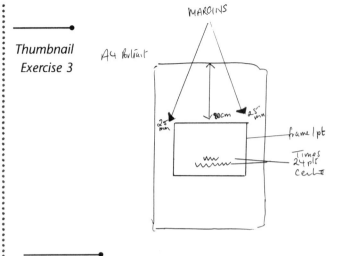

Move the I-beam after line 4 and click to insert

and

On the next line type

Lecturer in Public Relations

One blank line should also be removed between this last line and 'Video Show' to unify the contents of the notice.

Use the **rectangle drawing tool** at 1 pt to place a frame from margin to margin, making sure there is 10 mm of white space above and below the text.

The whole notice is to be placed centrally on the page. Select the frame and the text, zoom out and, using the rulers at the side of the screen, place the notice so that the frame starts at 80 mm down the page. **Save As** Dirnot3.???. **Print** one copy.

DIRECTORS' MEETING
Room 14 - 2pm
Chaired by Martin Hussey
Leading Market Research Officer
and
Lecturer in Public Relations

Video Show at 3.30 pm in Theatre

▼ EXERCISE 4
ADJUSTING TEXT STYLE AND ALIGNMENT

In this exercise you will learn how to

1 **recall a file**

2 **delete text and add text**

3 **add a graphic feature (a 4 pt line)**

4 **remove a frame and add another**

5 **adapt a text style from normal to italic**

6 **move a text block, frame and graphic line to centralise a notice on page, using rulers as a guide**

Recall Dirnot3.???. Remove the frame by selecting it with the text tool and using **Delete** from the Edit menu, or press the **Delete** key on the keypad with the Number Lock off.

Change the alignment of the line beginning 'Video' via the Type Specifications dialog box, by selecting **Centre** from Alignment.

Insert the following text below 'Theatre'.

MAKING YOUR COMPANY PROSPER

The type style is italic, so select **Italic** from the Type Style possibilities.

Draw a 1 pt frame around this line.

Insert the following text.

Tickets for the video presentation can be obtained free of charge from the Admissions Office

Use body text of 12 pts for this line and select **Centre** from Alignment.

Draw a 4 pt graphic line under 'Directors' Meeting', using the horizontal line tool. If you engage the shift key you *restrain* the line to be perfectly parallel.*

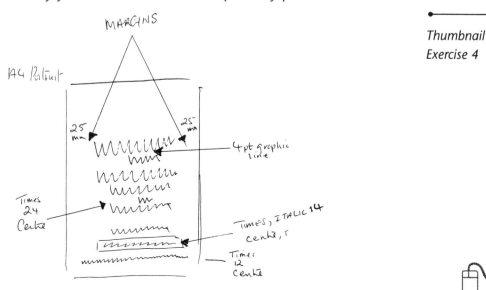

Thumbnail
Exercise 4

*Text style with rules combined is taught in Exercise 9

This notice has developed vertically and should now be moved up the page.

Use **Select All** from the Edit menu. Use the text tool to move the whole document up 20 mm.

Save As Dirnot4.???. **Print** one copy.

DIRECTORS' MEETING

Room 14 - 2pm

Chaired by Martin Hussey

Leading Market Research Officer

and

Lecturer in Public Relations

Video Show at 3.30 pm in Theatre

MAKING YOUR COMPANY PROSPER

Tickets for the video presentation can be obtained free of charge from the Admissions Office

▼ EXERCISE 5
CONSOLIDATION OF LAST FOUR EXERCISES

In this exercise you will

1 input text

2 create text styles

3 highlight and select styles

Provide a clear screen by clicking on **New** in the File menu, accept defaults and **OK**. Ensure that rulers are on, usually in Preferences, and choose View, Actual or 75%.

Using the **text tool**, type the following information straight onto the page at the top left, pressing **Enter** after each line.

Information on Contracts

A Seminar on this topic will be held

within the next two weeks

at

Holbein House Dublin 4

Delegates are asked to sign the attendance sheet in Main Office

Check the accuracy of the text and correct if necessary.

Still using the text tool, **highlight** line 1.

Create the following text specification from the Type or Paragraph menu.

Name	Inform
Size	24 pts and **Bold** from the Type Style options
Font	Times Roman
Alignment	Centre

This line will move to the centre in the chosen size and typeface when **Inform** is selected in the Type Style list.

Highlight line 2.

Create the following text specification from the Type or Paragraph menu.

Name	Seminar
Size	18 pts
Font	Times Roman
Alignment	Centre

This line will appear in the centre under line 1 when **Seminar** is selected from the Type Style list.

Highlight line 3 and click on **Seminar** in specification box, giving it the same characteristics as line 2.

Highlight line 4.

Create the following text specification from the Type or Paragraph menu.

Name	Small
Size	14 pts

Font	Times Roman
Alignment	Centre

This, too, will move into position under line 3 after selecting **Small** from the Type Style list.

Highlight line 5.

Select **Seminar** from the type specification list and this will take on the same attributes.

Highlight line 6.

Select **Small** from the type specification list to give it the attributes of line 4.

Return to full view and, placing the cursor on the first character of line 1, press **Enter** enough times to place the notice centrally on the vertical plane (approximately 6 times). Adjust vertically if necessary.

Save As Contract.??? (if not already saved, in which case just **Save**), with the appropriate extension and in the correct directory. **Print** from the File menu.

Thumbnail Exercise 5

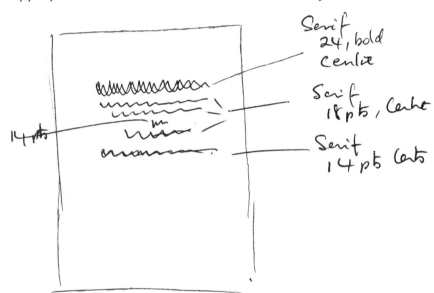

Information on Contracts

A Seminar on this topic will be held
within the next two weeks

at

Holbein House Dublin 4

Delegates are asked to sign the attendance sheet in Main Office

▼ EXERCISE 6
RECALLING LAST DOCUMENT TO COPY AND PASTE AFTER EDITING

In this exercise you will

1 **recall a file**

2 **add and delete text**

3 **highlight and select styles**

4 **create other text styles**

5 **copy and paste text**

Recall Contract.???. Insert the I-beam before 'Information' and type

Specialist

Delete 'within the next two weeks' and insert

on Wednesday at 7 00 pm
Before 'Dublin 4' insert
Donnybrook Avenue
After the address insert
Tel 7172766

Delete 'Delegates' and insert

Those wishing to attend

Insert

Ms Emelda Morgan will be available on a dedicated line to answer your questions after the Seminar on

Highlight the telephone number.
From the Edit menu choose **Copy**.

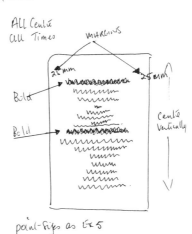

*Thumbnail
Exercise 6*

Insert the I-beam below the last line and point to Edit and then **Paste**.

The telephone number will be repeated accurately.

Insert the following text.

or by writing to her at

Highlight 'Holbein House Donnybrook Avenue Dublin 4' (lines 5 and 6)
Point to Edit and select **Copy**.

Place the I-beam after the last line and point to Edit and select **Paste**.

The address will appear.

The text specification for 'Ms Emelda Morgan' is the same as Inform.

Highlight the name and select **Inform** from the palette. **Save As** Contrac2.??? and **Print**.

Specialist Information on Contracts

A Seminar on this topic will be held

on Wednesday at 7 00 pm

at

Holbein House

Donnybrook Avenue Dublin 4

Tel 7172766

Those wishing to attend are asked to sign the attendance sheet in Main Office

Ms Emelda Morgan

will be available on a dedicated line to answer

your questions after the Seminar on

Tel 7172766

or by

writing to her at

Holbein House

Donnybrook Ave Dublin 4

▼ EXERCISE 7
CAPTION AND GRAPHIC ADDED TO LAST FILE

In this exercise you will

1 **recall a file**

2 **add and delete text**

3 **adapt a type specification**

4 **draw a frame**

5 **place a caption beneath a frame**

6 **position the elements of the notice pleasingly**

Recall Contrac2.???. Remove the emboldening from the first line by selecting Text and Type Styles and **Normal**.

Delete all the text after 'Ms Emelda Morgan'. Insert the following names.

Alan Harris

Ms Julia O'Reilly

Desmond Magee

Edit the text specification Morgan to be **Left Aligned** and use it for the names. Below these names input

will be speakers at the Seminar

Use the **Small** specification, adapted for left alignment.

On the right, opposite the names, draw a rectangle 40 mm wide and 50 mm deep to eventually frame a photograph of Ms Emelda Morgan.

Beneath this frame, input the following caption.

Ms Emelda Morgan

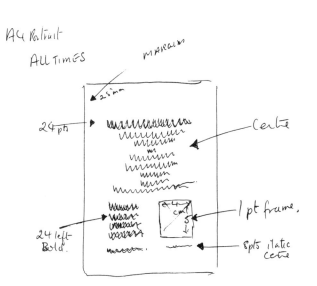

Thumbnail
Exercise 7

For this caption, create the following text specification.

Name	Photo
Size	8 pts
Font	Serif Italic
Alignment	Centre

To import the image, choose **Place** or **Import** from the File menu. If you have installed the disk that came with this book, when the dialog box appears, select the C drive, Image.96 directory and the file emelda.pcx. Click twice on the file, or click on **OK** and your cursor will be 'loaded' with the image. By clicking in the frame reserved for the photograph the image will appear. Its size may have to be adjusted to fit exactly. Use the 'handles' at the lower corners of the image to make it larger or smaller.

Save As Contrac3.??? and **Print**.

Specialist Information on Contracts

A Seminar on this topic will be held
on Wednesday at 7 00 pm
at
Holbein House
Donnybrook Avenue
Dublin 4
Tel 7172766

Those wishing to attend are asked to sign the attendance sheet in Main Office

Ms Emelda Morgan
Alan Harris
Ms Julia O'Reilly
Desmond Magee

Ms Emelda Morgan

will be speakers at the Seminar

▼ EXERCISE 8

USING A WORD PROCESSOR, SAVING AS ASCII, IMPORTING TO DOCUMENT

In this exercise you will

1 **import text from a word processor and use a spell checker**

2 **separate unformatted text into paragraphs**

3 **select sans serif typeface for a main text**

4 **position material vertically on the page with Select All**

Using a word processor, type the following text.

ATHLETICS

Participants are reminded of the following

During the competition you are required to leave all personal belongings in the changing rooms under lock and key. You may not take any items whatsoever to the field.

You are to assemble in the area marked on your card 10 minutes before the race for which you are entered. Your final registration will take place there and you will be given an identification number which must be used in all references to your race.

P J Herbert — Athletics Committee

If your word processing package has a Spell Checker, use it to correct any typographical or spelling errors. **Save As** Athlet.???. (Be sure to use the extension and format your package will accept. ASCII will be universally accepted by all desktop publishing packages, but you should confirm whether ASC, TXT, or any other extension is required.) Save this text file in an appropriate directory.

It is wise to keep the prepared text and completed documents from the DTP package in separate directories, but note that good work practice requires a *file name* that identifies both these items for easy assembly later. The recommendations in this book for file names will follow this principle.

IMPORTING TEXT INTO A DOCUMENT

Open your desktop publishing package. Choose **New** in the File menu and **OK** to accept the defaults. Select **Place**, or **Import** from the File menu. When the dialog box appears, select the correct drive, directory and file extension (whether ASCII or any other) — the one you used to store your typed text above.

Your cursor will be **loaded** with the text selected, and by clicking in the top left of your page you will observe the text **flow** into it.

If you set out your text in a word processor with a separate heading and into paragraphs as shown above, then you will not have to do that now. However, if it loads

as one paragraph, separate it now by pressing **Enter** after the heading and paragraphs shown above.

TO TYPESET THIS NOTICE

Highlight the heading. Create the following specifications.

Name	Main
Size	20 pts
Font	Sans Serif (Helvetica)
Alignment	Left

Highlight the second line and ascribe the following attributes.

Name	Secondary
Size	18 pts
Font	Sans Serif
Alignment	Left

Highlight both paragraphs and ascribe the following attributes.

Name	Paras
Size	14 pts
Font	Sans Serif
Alignment	Left

Enter another blank line after 'your race' and before 'P J Herbert'.

Highlight this last line and use **Secondary** from the Type Specification list to define it.

Adjust the vertical position of the whole announcement in either of the following ways.

1   place the cursor (I-beam) just at the A of 'ATHLETICS' and press **Enter** 4 or 5 times

or

2   select the text block and move it as a whole down the page.

Use the **ruler guides** at the left side of the screen to place the text centrally.

You should have been saving your work regularly, but, if you have not, **Save As** Athlet.??? and **Print** from the File menu.

Thumbnail Exercise 8

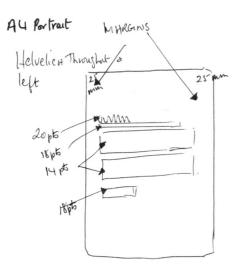

ATHLETICS

Participants are reminded of the following

During the competition you are required to leave all personal belongings in the changing rooms under lock and key. You may not take any items whatsoever to the field.

You are to assemble in the area marked on your card 10 minutes before the race for which you are entered. Your final registration will take place there and you will be given an identification number which must be used in all references to your race.

PJ Herbert - Athletics Committee

▼ EXERCISE 9

ADAPTING PAGE SETUP AND LEADING

In this exercise you will

1 **change the margin width**

2 **create indented paragraphs**

3 **change the leading from the default**

4 **place rule under text from type style options**

Recall Athlet.???. Change the margins either in the Page Setup menu or by altering the text box dimensions. Set left and right margins at 35 mm.

To adapt the type style to the new requirements of indented paragraph style, return to the dialog box Paras, which you used to set up the style for the text, and here you should find the **Indents** options.

Input 5 mm for the first line. This is an edit of the original type style. **Highlight** this section of the notice and select the edit style **Paras**, and the paragraph style changes to indented.

Leading is the term used to measure the distance between the baseline of one line and the baseline of the one above or below it. This distance is usually the height in points of the characters plus one fifth, therefore the standard leading is 120%. This figure can be altered to enable copy fitting to be successful or, as in this case, to make

the text more attractive and readable by enlarging the distance between each line. Here with 14 pts text, 18 pts is standard. Increase the leading through the paragraph dialog box to 22 pts.

Thumbnail Exercise 9

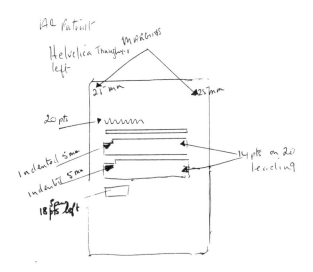

The heading style Main is changed to include a 1 pt rule below this paragraph through the same group of dialog boxes where **Rules** is an option. Some packages must have a text or column width chosen — select text width here. Choosing this adaptation to a style ensures that the rule is part of the text and moves with it, whatever layout changes may occur.

Rules with text is also preferable to using the underscore, because there is no variation in line width and often the underscore interferes with the overall appearance of the document, as it is too close to the baseline of the characters and often cuts descenders. **Save As** Athlet2.??? and **Print**.

ATHLETICS

Participants are reminded of the following

During the competition you are required to leave all personal belongings in the changing rooms under lock and key. You may not take any items whatsoever to the field.

You are to assemble in the area marked on your card 10 minutes before the race for which you are entered. Your final registration will take place there and you will be given an identification number which must be used in all references to your race.

PJ Herbert - Athletics Committee

▼ EXERCISE 10
FILL FRAME, REMOVE LINE, ADD BULLETS

In this exercise you will

1 draw a frame and fill with 10% shading

2 remove some type style features

3 separate text into shorter paragraphs and precede them with bullets

4 change a frame line to none

Recall Athlet2.???. Selecting the **rectangle drawing tool**, draw a rectangle 10 mm deep and from left to right margin. While this is still selected, use the **Fill** option and 10% density. Select the frame again and change the frame line to **None**.

Copy and **Paste** the filled rectangle. Drag this to the foot of the notice.

Drag the word 'ATHLETICS' onto the filled rectangle, making it centred.

Drag the last line onto the second filled rectangle, making it centred.

Return the leading to 18 pts in the two long paragraphs and remove the indentations.

Divide the two main paragraphs into separate sentences (four in total).

Create a further type style.

Name	Bullet
Size	14 pts
Alignment	Left

Selecting a simple bullet from the Paragraph option dialog box, apply this to each of the four sentences. **Save As** Athlet3.??? and **Print**.

Thumbnail
Exercise 10

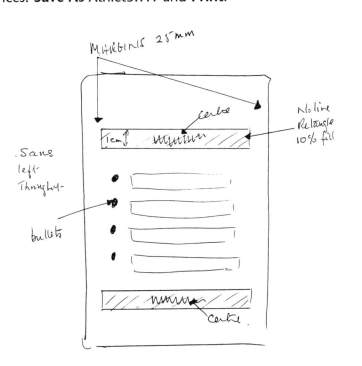

ATHLETICS

Participants are reminded of the following

- During the competition you are required to leave all personal belongings in the changing rooms under lock and key.

- You may not take any items whatsoever to the field.

- You are to assemble in the area marked on your card 10 minutes before the race for which you are entered.

- Your final registration will take place there and you will be given an identification number which must be used in all references to your race.

PJ Herbert - Athletics Committee

▼ EXERCISE 11

LANDSCAPE ORIENTATION

In this exercise you will

1 **work in landscape orientation**
2 **import prepared text from a word processor**
3 **assess the vertical placement of this orientation**

Prepare the following text in your word processor.

EXTRA MURAL COURSES

THE MIDLANDS COLLEGE

Enrolment Procedures

Between September 2nd and 27th you can enrol at the Adult Education Office from 9 am – 5 pm. You will be given a receipt on payment of the fees. Please be certain to keep this receipt with you when on Campus as you may be asked for it at any time.

Information and Advice on all Extra Mural Courses will be available from tutors during the week September 2nd to 6th in the Jackson Hall from 6.30 pm to 9.30 pm each evening.

The Bursar and Registrar Midlands College

You should proofread your input thoroughly and if you have a Spell Checker use it as well. **Save As** Exmur.??? in the correct directory, ensuring that the extension is correct for importation to your DTP package (ASCII is certain to import).

In the DTP package, clear your screen with **New**, but observe the dialog box that appears. Select **Wide** or **Landscape**, with margins of 25 mm all round, and **OK**. Your page dimensions will now be 297 mm across and 210 mm down, giving you a page that is wider than it is deep.

Import the file Exmur.??? by selecting **Import** or **Place** from the File menu. Click on the file name and **OK**. Your text will appear and, by clicking within the margins at the top left of the page, your text will flow in. (Refer to Exercise 8 to revise details of the importing procedure.)

Make sure you are in a close view; Actual or 75% is ideal. Select the text tool and separate the two headings by pressing **Enter** after each line, if your text has not imported as it was typed.

Highlight the first line and create the following text specification.

Name	Extra
Size	30 pts
Font	Serif (Palatino is used here)
Alignment	Centre

Highlight the second line and attribute the following specifications.

Name	College
Size	18 pts
Font	Sans Serif
Alignment	Centre

Highlight the third line and use the following specifications.

Name	Proced
Size	24 pts
Font	Serif (Palatino is used here)
Alignment	Centre

Select the whole of the text from 'Between' to 'evening' and set the following attributes.

Name	Para
Size	14 pts
Font	Sans Serif
Alignment	Left

Break this text into two paragraphs by inserting the cursor after 'any time' and press **Enter**.

Highlight the last line and set the following attributes.

Name	Burs
Size	14 pts
Font	Sans Serif
Alignment	Right

Change to full view to assess the vertical placement and overall look of this document. Adjust the position of the whole text in relation to the page depth as before, using the cursor or the frame in which the text was placed to move it further down.

Save As Exmur.??? in the appropriate directory. **Print** 1 copy.

Thumbnail
Exercise 11

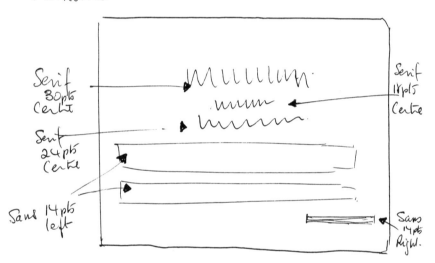

EXTRA MURAL COURSES

THE MIDLANDS COLLEGE

Enrolment Procedures

Between September 2nd and 27th you can enrol at the Adult Education Office from 9 am - 5 pm. You will be given a receipt on payment of the fees. Please be certain to keep this receipt with you on Campus as you may be asked for it at any time.

Information and Advice on all Extra Mural Courses will be available from tutors during the week September 2nd to 6th in the Jackson Hall from 6. 30 pm to 9.30 pm each evening.

The Bursar and Registrar Midlands College

▼ EXERCISE 12
ADAPT PAGE SETUP AND ADD A FORM TO LAST FILE

In this exercise you will

1 **change margins**

2 **insert a new paragraph**

3 **adapt a created type style**

4 **use the drawing tool and a broken line to develop a tear-off form**

5 **input text using the tab key**

Recall Exmur.???. This announcement will look better with wider margins; 50 mm is the ideal choice left and right, with 15 mm top and bottom. (You can, instead of altering the page setup dialog box in File menu, adjust the text box to be narrower by 50 mm than it appeared in the first draft of this example.)

Insert a new paragraph after 'any time' by pressing **Enter** and typing

Admission to all classes is on production of your receipt

You should make the following changes as well.

Highlight the first line and select Type Style from the Text or Type menu and click on **Bold**.

Highlight the new paragraph and, in the Type Style menu, select **Italic**.

Set **Bold** in the same way for the line beginning 'The Bursar'.

Insert a new paragraph after the last line and type

Having filled in the attached form cut along the dotted line and leave it into Reception. This will ensure a personal interview with your tutor at the specified time.

Use the line tool to draw from left to right margin. Select the broken line from the line options.

Type the following details onto the electronic page, using the tab key and the preset positions to space out the sections across the page.

NAME   PREFERRED EVENING

COURSE NO   PREFERRED TIME

TUTOR

Create a new type style as follows.

Name	Data
Size	10 pts
Font	Sans Serif
Alignment	Left

Select the **Data** type style for these parts of the form and the paragraph just inserted before the line.

Use the graphic line at 1 pt to determine where users will fill in the form, copying and pasting this where appropriate. Zoom out and adjust the document's elements to be well placed vertically.

Save As Exmur2.???. **Print** one copy.

*Thumbnail
Exercise 12*

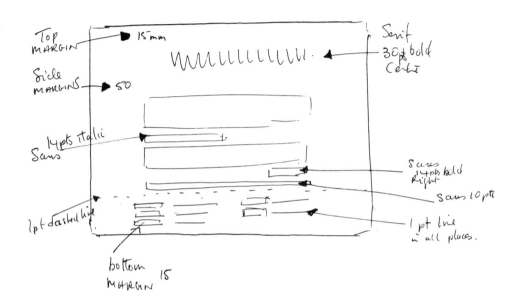

EXTRA MURAL COURSES

THE MIDLANDS COLLEGE

Enrolment Procedures

Between September 2nd and 27th you can enrol at the Adult Education Office from 9 am - 5 pm. You will be given a receipt on payment of the fees. Please be certain to keep this receipt with you on Campus as you may be asked for it at any time.

Admission to all classes is on production of your receipt

Information and Advice on all Extra Mural Courses will be available from tutors during the week September 2nd to 6th in the Jackson Hall from 6.30 pm to 9.30 pm each evening.

The Bursar and Registrar Midlands College

Having filled in the attached form cut along the dotted line and leave it into Reception. This will ensure a personal interview with your tutor at the specified time.

- -

NAME _____   PREFERRED EVENING _____

COURSE NO _____   PREFERRED TIME _____

TUTOR _____

▼ EXERCISE 13
A REPORT COVER

In this exercise you will

1   **use graphic features for effect**

2   **use varying weights of text**

3   **place text in a rounded box**

4   **use white space to advantage**

From File choose **New**, accept A4 portrait and select margins, left 35 mm, with right and top and bottom 25 mm. The wide left-hand margin will ensure that the report and cover can be bound and all the text still be visible.

Using the example to copy from, type the text of this cover in the top left corner of the page, creating the separate paragraphs shown by pressing **Enter** after each line.

The following are the specifications.

Line one

Name	Build
Size	36 pts
Font	Serif
Alignment	Left

Line two

Name	Report
Size	18 pts
Font	Sans Serif (Helvetica or Swiss), bold
Alignment	Left

Lines three and four

Select **Report** from the type specification list, removing the emboldening.

The line giving the author's name

Name	Author
Size	14 pts
Font	Sans Serif
Alignment	Left

The text in the rounded box also has the same attributes as the last line (Author).

The text starts 80 mm down from the top of the page, with two paragraph entries between each.

The rounded box has a .5 pt line and the most rounded corners, chosen from the corner options.

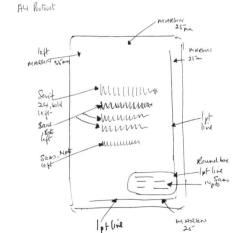

Thumbnail
Exercise 13

With the **horizontal line tool** from the toolbox, draw a 1pt line (you may have to keep the shift key down to maintain a perfectly straight line), following the right-hand margin. Draw another line over the margin across the bottom of the page. The box and the text are placed approximately 10 mm up and in from these lines.

BUILDINGS VALUATIONS 1996

REPORT TO FINANCIAL COMMITTEE

Survey of Suburban Area 4

Undertaken January - March

By Joseph Moriarty

Issued April 1996

To   Financial Committee

From   Valuation Department

▼ EXERCISE 14
USING GRAPHICS TOOLS TO MAKE A DIAGRAM

In this exercise you will

1 use the ellipse, rectangle and line drawing tools

2 use the fill feature

3 import an image from a library of images or another source

4 create text to suit individual needs

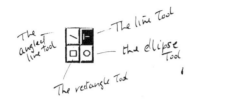

Tools

Start with a **New** default page. Draw a rectangle with the **rectangle tool**, 80 mm deep by 70 mm wide, into which the graphic will be imported. Place this rectangle 70 mm down the page and at the right-hand margin.

Draw an ellipse 60 mm long and 15 mm deep.

Use a medium to light fill (10 to 20%).

Copy and **Paste** this shape three more times. Drag each copy to a position at least 50 mm to the left and below the rectangle for the image.

Use a 1 pt angled line for each of the lines and place two small angled lines at their ends for the arrow heads, if your package does not have a Line Ends facility.

You will have a library of images, either as part of the DTP package, or provided by your tutor, or on the disk which came with this book. (For practice purposes it does not really matter what the image is.) Import the image by selecting **Import** or **Place** or **Import Picture** from the File menu. From that dialog box select the correct drive, A, if the images are stored on separate disks, and the correct extension. PCX is almost universal, while TIFF and BMP are also quite likely to be compatible with your package.

Select **OK** and either click in the box you have drawn or the image will appear on the page or paste board ready to be dragged into position and size with the pointer.

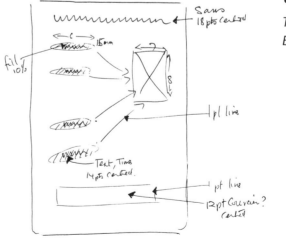

Thumbnail Exercise 14

The text is typed as separate text blocks, either into the ellipses or on the paste board, and positioned in them (Times, 14 pts, centred alignment).

The title is 18 pts, Helvetica and centred.

If you are using this cover for your course material, fill in the appropriate details in the box at the foot of the page which is framed in a 1 pt line width; the text here can be any suitable size and position.

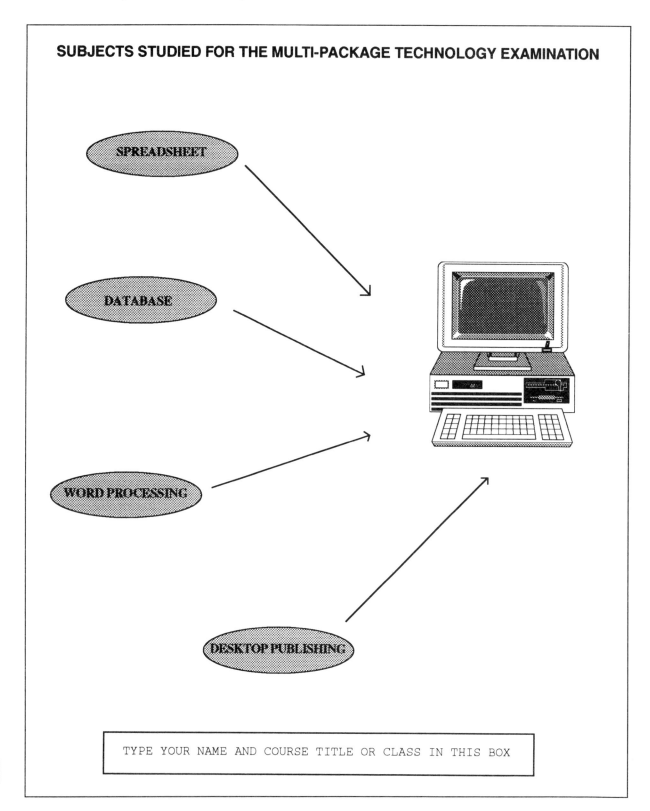

▼ EXERCISE 15
A FORM (MULTIPLE PASTE)

In this exercise you will

1	**copy and paste multiple copies**
2	**use the rulers across and down the page to place accurately**

Your package may not produce the '£' sign, even though installed for the UK keyboard. This can be overcome by inputting it as a non-keyboard character where this sign is needed. You must put the cursor where you wish the '£' to be produced and, making sure the Number Lock is not on, keep the **Alt** key down and press the numbers 1, 5 and 6 on the keypad (not the top row of the keyboard).

The copy and paste feature is in the Edit menu. Note that using **Copy** puts data into the clipboard (a temporary store) and **Paste** returns a copy of the data to a selected position, or on the page for you to position where required. **Clear**, however, removes the selected data completely and it cannot be returned. (**Cut** can return data from the clipboard as it removes the data to be placed elsewhere.)

For this exercise, it would be wise to retain the unit of measure at centimetres and millimetres (this can usually be chosen from Units in the Preferences submenu).

Start with a **New** default page. Select the **horizontal line tool** from the toolbox.

60 mm from the top of the page, draw a line from margin to margin.

Make sure the line width is ·5 pt. You can check or select this width from the Draw, Line or Graphic menu under **Line**, or select the narrowest your package provides.

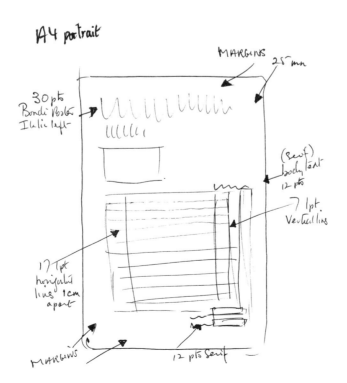

Thumbnail
Exercise 15

Copy once and **Paste** this line 16 times (or use multiple paste if available) and move each line into position 10 mm below the last. You should work in the closest possible view to accurately position the lines.

Draw a vertical line 160 mm long down the side of the page at the left-hand margin. **Copy** and **Paste** it three times. Place two before the £ column and one at the right-hand margin.

Draw one vertical line 150 mm long after the £ columns and **Copy** and **Paste** it once more for the other pence column.

Draw one box 10 mm x 40 mm with a 1 pt line which is copied and pasted for 'Vat' and 'Total'.

Draw one box 25 mm by 60 mm for the address.

In body text, in the first column, type

Quantity

and, where shown, type

£

and

p

The type specifications for the rest of the text are as follows, though any similar type style is acceptable.

Supplier's name	30 pts, Bodoni Poster Italic, left aligned
Order form and address	12 pts, left aligned
Send to	12 pts, right aligned, bold

'Vat' and 'Total' lines are in body text and left aligned.

Always return to full page view so that you can adjust the overall look (with **Select All**, Edit menu, if it is a general placement) and the detail of relationships between parts of a document, by moving the relevant frames slightly. **Save As** Danform.??? in the correct directory and **Print**.

DANIELS CITY SUPPLIES LTD

ORDER FORM   **Send to**

39 Almartin Road
Cross Glen

Quantity		£	p	£	p
		Unit		Total	

VAT

Total value of order

▼ Exercise 16

Importing Images from Clip Art Library or from Scanned Image Provided

In this exercise you will

1   **place rectangles precisely**

2   **copy and paste**

3   **import images**

4   **insert captions**

This is a simple copy and paste routine for the frames and the caption boxes.

Ensure that your measurements are set to centimetres and millimetres for this exercise (in Preferences). You should also set **Snap to Guides** to be on.

You are recommended to **Save As** Art.??? as soon as the grid is set up and continue saving regularly (every few minutes is wise).

You will find a grid very useful for this exercise. If your package has **guide lines** and they can be taken with the pointer from the side and top rulers, set them up as follows:

Horizontally at 130, 140, 250 and 260 mm (indicating just the base of each box) and vertically at 70 and 140 mm.

This provides the framework in which to draw the boxes and then **Place** or **Import** the pictures into these.

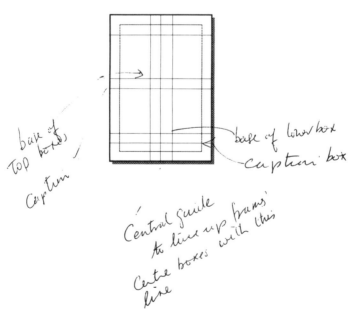

Without guide lines, you can draw frames to these measurements and set them centrally on the page, using the grey line which plots the pointer movements within the rulers as an accurate guide. Also zoom in and out to check the overall look and see the exact placement of all the elements, whichever method you use.

The graphics are in boxes measuring 70 mm wide by 80 mm deep.

The captions are in boxes measuring 70 mm wide by 7 mm deep.

Draw the top pair of rectangles. **Copy** and **paste** them to the second part of the grid structure.

If you wish the graphics to appear directly in the first frame, you may have to select it before you choose **Place, Import Picture,** or **Import Text and Picture** from the File menu. When the dialog box appears, you should select the correct drive and directory in which the graphic file is to be found and the appropriate extension. Click twice on the file name, or once to select it and **OK.**

The pointer will either be loaded with the image, or the name of the file will be in the file list. The image is likely to appear in the box if you have already selected it. You can drag the pointer to the box and resize it if necessary by grasping the handles and making it larger or smaller. Repeat this procedure for the second image.

In the frames for the captions, type the information given (body text 12 pt Roman, centred, with italic type style).

25 mm above the frames, type this heading

The Winning Entries in the Art Exhibition

The specifications to be used are Times Roman, 24 pts, with centred alignment. Check the overall look of the document, adjusting the positions of text and boxes with the use of the rulers and guides. **Save As** Art.??? and **Print.**

The caption boxes are 3 mm below the picture frame. The line width for all frames is ·5.

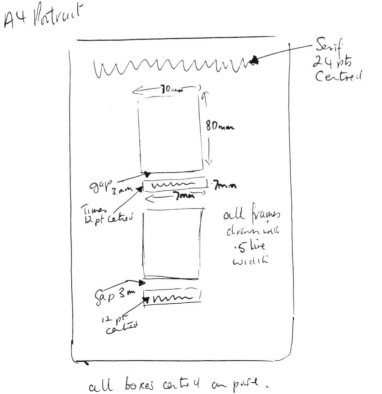

Thumbnail

Exercise 16

The Winning Entries in the Art Exhibition

Still Life by Joseph O'Grady

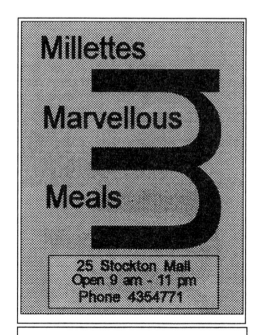

Dynamic Poster by Helen Stephens

▼ EXERCISE 17
CREATING A LOGO WITH GRAPHICS TOOLS WITHIN DESKTOP PUBLISHING PACKAGE

In this exercise you will

1   **use most of the drawing tools to create a logo**

2   **select a feature to be Sent to Back or vice versa**

3   **fill with a variety of densities**

4   **copy and paste**

Students should get general practice with the drawing tools selected from the toolbox before starting the exercise. You should become familiar with drawing circles, ellipses, rectangles, squares, horizontal and angled lines. Your drawing line is best at 1 pt or the package default.

Once familiar with the drawing tools, draw the following shapes to the dimensions given. Remember to size accurately by moving into the page much closer. Actual, 200%, or 400% if available, will make it easier to draw shapes to the specific sizes required.

Draw

one circle with 12 mm radius

three ellipses

a. 18 mm long and 6 mm deep

b. 25 mm long and 15 mm deep

c. 30 mm long and 18 mm deep

one square with dimensions of 18 mm each side

one line, vertical, 18 mm long

one line, angled approximately 40°, 6 mm long.

These shapes may be anywhere on the page. To assemble them, select each one with the pointer to show handles. Then, pointing to the outline of the shape, drag it to the required place. Deselect this shape and select another, positioning it carefully in relation to the last.

You can ensure that the circle, for instance, is placed to hide the further side of the ellipse by selecting the ellipse and selecting **Send to Back** in the Draw, Graphic, or Element menu.

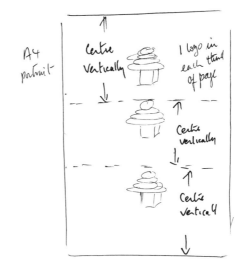

Thumbnail
Exercise 17

By pointing to any of the fully enclosed shapes, they can be shaded with a density of **fill**, usually from the same menu. For this exercise, 50% or less is best. Often text is written inside shaded areas, but it loses its impact if the background is too dark, so keep to low densities. (Exercises in other parts of the book have text placed in shaded areas, and low density shading is used so that it can be read.)

The shapes you have assembled in the exercise will be used later in the course to provide a logo for a company's stationery, so **Save As** Logo.???.

The components of the logo should be 'grouped' if your DTP package provides for this. If not, the logo can be created in a paint or drawing program, grouped there and saved as a PCX or other suitable file. It can then be resized for use later in the course.

When you have created one satisfactory logo, **Copy** and **Paste** it twice, placing each in a third of the page length. **Print** one copy.

▼ EXERCISE 18
AN A5 FORM

In this exercise you will

1   **set up an A5 page**

2   **use text with rules as a paragraph feature**

3   **use guides to help place text boxes**

4   **print using crop marks**

At **New** from the File menu, select **A5** and **Landscape** (margins 10 mm all round).

To make it easy to place the text, the page can be divided equally by creating 2 columns with a 5 mm gutter. **Snap to Guides** should be on as well.

Guide lines or a grid should be set up at 20 mm intervals to aid in aligning the elements.

The following text specifications should be created for the style palette.

Head	Palatino, 16 pts, centre, with line text width and bold
Data	Times New Roman, 14 pts, left

Create each text item as a separate entity, so that it can be placed accurately and manoeuvred easily.

A 1 pt line the width of the first column is needed for the 'Name' line, and after that a shorter line can be drawn, copied and pasted 7 times and placed after each text block.

Save As Formap1.???. In the Print dialog box, ensure the orientation is **Landscape**.

Check the box for **crop marks**, as these will identify the exact area the form will occupy on the A4 sheet. In a professional print situation, the crop marks indicate where the paper will be cut.

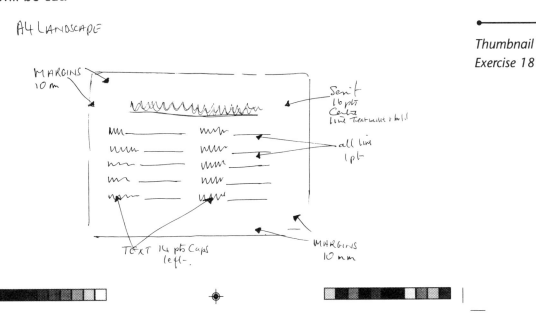

*Thumbnail
Exercise 18*

FACULTY APPLICATION AND REFERENCES 2ND YEAR

NAME ———————————	I ST YEAR SUBJECTS ———————
STUDENT NUMBER ———————	AVERAGE GRADES ———————
YEAR TUTOR ———————	HIGHEST GRADE ———————
FIRST CHOICE ———————	PERSONAL TUTOR ———————
SECOND CHOICE ———————	CONTACT PHONE NO ———————

▼ Exercise 19
Amended A5 Form

In this exercise you will

1 **edit the existing form**

2 **copy and paste graphic features**

Recall the last exercise, Formap1.???. Remove the last three text items and their lines.

Using **Head** type style, insert

Official Use Only

Drag this text below the last item.

Insert

Passed all

Resit

Tutor approves

as separate text boxes, dragging them to line up with the rest of the form. Use the body text default that is part of the style palette for all the text in this section.

Use the drawing tools to create a rectangle 30 mm x 10 mm which is divided in half by a vertical line.

Place

Yes

and

No

in the box.

Some packages allow users to draw a marquee around a group of objects, instead of individually selecting them. Draw a marquee around the box with the pointer, if your package allows, and **Copy** and **Paste** it twice more. Drag each one into place beside the text item.

Remember to zoom out to check the overall placement of your elements and adjust any detail by changing view to 200% or more.

Save As Formap2.???. **Print** with the same choices selected in the dialog box as in Exercise 18.

A4 LANDSCAPE

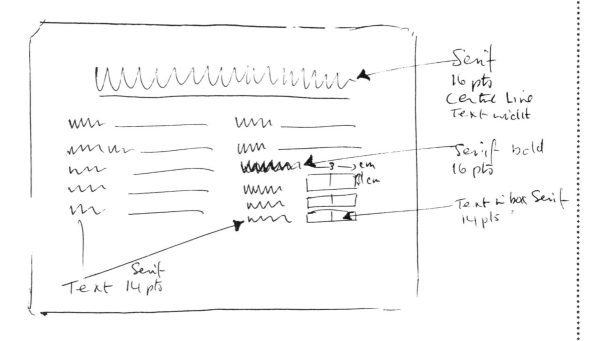

Serif
16 pts
Central Line
Text width

Serif bold
16 pts

Text in box Serif
14 pts

Serif
Text 14 pts

FACULTY APPLICATION AND REFERENCES 2ND YEAR

NAME _____   1ST YEAR SUBJECTS _____

STUDENT NUMBER _____   AVERAGE GRADES _____

Official Use Only

YEAR TUTOR _____   Passed all

Yes	No

FIRST CHOICE _____   Resit

Yes	No

SECOND CHOICE _____   Tutor approves

Yes	No

· PART TWO ·
FACTS, EXAMPLES AND EXERCISES

HORIZONTAL ALIGNMENT

Horizontal alignment is an important consideration right from the start of any skill building in desktop publishing. This term refers to the placement of text in relation to the width of the space it occupies.

In the examples shown here, the first one has **left** alignment, where the left margin is straight and the lines end unevenly. In the second example, the alignment is **right**, so that the right margin is perfectly straight and the left uneven.

There are layouts that require **centred** alignment (shown in the third example), where both margins are uneven. The fourth example has **justified** alignment, where both margins are even because extra, small and usually undetected spaces are inserted between the words. In all these examples, hyphenation has been turned off. Switching it on will decrease the amount of space inserted in justified text, but in narrow text areas the hyphenation can be a distraction. In example 5, **force justify** has been used to make the text fit a specific width as exactly as possible. Text only needs to be force justified in large point sizes, usually in headlines.

From these examples, you can see another feature which helps to display text to advantage. The text within the box has been given a **standoff**, which prevents it touching the frame and becoming difficult to read. In some packages it is the frame which has an internal standoff. An external standoff is also needed around frames which contain images, to keep the text away from the frame. It is important to remember that all text needs some white space around it to be easily read.

PARAGRAPH CHARACTERISTICS

There are three types of paragraph styles in common use. In example 1, the **indented** paragraph style is illustrated, where the first line starts in from the margin. In this case, 10 mm was chosen for emphasis, while the default is 5 mm. It is used to identify the beginning of a new paragraph when a 'space after' is not defined, otherwise there would be no indication of a new paragraph when it finished at the end of a line.

In the second example, **block** style is shown, where every line starts at the left margin. There is, of course, space after the paragraphs for easy identification.

The third style, **hanging indented**, has the first line only at the margin and all following lines beginning to the right. This paragraph style would not be used in continuous text, but it is useful for reports, and informative articles in which topics need to be found easily. This style lends itself to numbering and paragraph subsections.

Apartments like these rarely come on the market. These have all been developed from a widely accepted formula that has sold well for the last four years but given individuality by being personalised for this site. This means that wherever possible, the living room has been placed to give the best view or the best light as a priority and the other rooms designed to lead from this while bedrooms are accessed from another direction.

Example 1 – Left aligned

Apartments like these rarely come on the market. These have all been developed from a widely accepted formula that has sold well for the last four years but given individuality by being personalised for this site. This means that wherever possible, the living room has been placed to give the best view or the best light as a priority and the other rooms designed to lead from this while bedrooms are accessed from another direction.

Example 2 – Right aligned

Horizontal alignment

Apartments like these rarely come on the market. These have all been developed from a widely accepted formula that has sold well for the last four years but given individuality by being personalised for this site. This means that wherever possible, the living room has been placed to give the best view or the best light as a priority and the other rooms designed to lead from this while bedrooms are accessed from another direction.

Example 3 – Centre aligned

Apartments like these rarely come on the market. These have all been developed from a widely accepted formula that has sold well for the last four years but given individuality by being personalised for this site. This means that wherever possible, the living room has been placed to give the best view or the best light as a priority and the other rooms designed to lead from this while bedrooms are accessed from another direction.

Example 4 – Justified aligned

P R O P E R T Y
DEVELOPMENTS

Example 5 – Here the alignment is Force Justified

There are some interesting points to note about paragraphing and hyphenation. Using justified text in example 4 has forced the spacing between words to become so wide that what are called 'rivers' appear through the text. This is a distraction to the reader, as well as being unattractive on the page, and should be removed by introducing **hyphenation**. Hyphenation is part of the paragraph style and can be turned on and off as part of the style specification.

In example 5, over-use of hyphenation has caused repeated occurrence of word separation and this, too, is to be avoided. It is a particular problem in very short lines and can sometimes be overcome, as in example 6, by changing the line length.

These examples show that only by practice and observation can users of desktop publishing packages come near to the professional typesetter. As you progress through the course, you will become more aware of ways to improve the appearance of your work, as well as becoming more proficient with the software.

Indented block paragraphs

James Joyce was a student of Philosophy and English at University College from 1899 to 1902. The old Physics Theatre of the University is located on the first floor of Number 85; it was in this room that Joyce gave his maiden speech to the Literary and Historical Society.

Joyce later used the Physics Theatre as a setting for an encounter in A Portrait of the Artist as a Young Man. In 1854 the newly established Catholic University of Ireland received its first students in Number 86 St Stephen's Green.

Example 1 – Indented paragraphs

In the late nineteenth century the stairhall of Number 85 was radically altered by an unsympathetic remodelling. During the course of the restoration programme the stairhall has been painstakingly returned to its wonderful eighteenth-century appearance.

An additional flight of stairs, inserted during the 1870's, has now been removed and the original ceiling level has been reinstated. During the course of restoration a curious lunette window was discovered above the stairhall's window.

Example 2 – Block paragraphs

*Hanging indented
paragraphs*

In the late nineteenth century the stairhall of Number 85 was radically altered by an unsympathetic remodelling. During the course of the restoration programme the stairhall has been painstakingly returned to its wonderful eighteenth-century appearance.

An additional flight of stairs, inserted during the 1870's, has now been removed and the original ceiling level has been reinstated. During the course of restoration a curious lunette window was discovered above the stairhall's window.

Example 3 – Hanging indented paragraphs

In the nineteenth century the stairhall of was radically altered by an unsympathetic remodelling. During the course of the restoration programme the stairhall has been painstakingly returned to its wonderful eighteenth-century appearance.

An additional flight of stairs, inserted during the 1870's, has been removed and the original ceiling level reinstated. During the course of restoration a lunette window was discovered above the stairhall's window.

Example 4 – Rivers of white in text that has been justified. Avoid this feature

*The effects of
hyphenation on
paragraphs*

In the nineteenth century the stairhall of was radically altered by an un-sympathetic remodelling. During the course of the restoration programme the stairhall has been painstakingly re-turned to its wonderful eighteenth-century appearance.

An additional flight of stairs, inserted during the 1870's, has been removed and the original ceiling level rein-stated. During the course of resto-ration a lunette window was discov-ered above the stairhall's window.

Example 5 – Hyphenation used in short line lengths becomes a hindrance to easy reading

In the nineteenth century the stairhall of was radically altered by an un-sympathetic remodelling. During the course of the restoration programme the stairhall has been painstakingly returned to its wonderful eighteenth-century appearance.

An additional flight of stairs, in-serted during the 1870's, has been removed and the original ceiling level reinstated. During the course of restoration a lunette window was discovered above the stairhall's window.

Example 6 – Hyphenation used in short line lengths in left aligned text reduces the incidence of word breaks

VERTICAL ALIGNMENT

The position of text within the space allotted to it is very important. The desktop publisher is concerned with the **vertical** and **horizontal alignment**.

In this exercise, you can replicate the examples by copying and pasting a square of 60 mm twice, with 20 mm between each square. You should type the text either in a word processor and then import it into each square, or type straight into the first square and copy, then paste the text into subsequent squares. All three have centred horizontal alignment, but they all have different vertical alignment.

In the first example, the **top** alignment is selected (from the paragraph characteristics), the second has **centred** vertical alignment, while the last has **bottom** vertical alignment. Make your page look exactly like this example. Save as Vertal.???.

PARAGRAPH SPACING

Text used so far has rarely required students to consider the space between paragraphs.

Essentially, desktop publishing accepts that a paragraph ends whenever the Enter key is used. To use the Enter key to start a new line is, therefore, inaccurate. Paragraph space is wider than leading, which is space between lines. In some cases, line ends are controlled by varying the width of the text block. Paragraphs should be indicated by pressing the Enter key once where the space between paragraphs has been set with a specific **space after** measurement. In most of the exercises in this book, 2 millimetres have been set after paragraphs.

Vertical alignment

Apartments like these rarely come on the market. These have all been developed from a widely accepted formula that has sold well for the last four years but given individuality by being personalised for this site.

Example 1 – Top alignment

Apartments like these rarely come on the market. These have all been developed from a widely accepted formula that has sold well for the last four years but given individuality by being personalised for this site.

Example 2 – Centred alignment

Apartments like these rarely come on the market. These have all been developed from a widely accepted formula that has sold well for the last four years but given individuality by being personalised for this site.

Example 3 – Bottom alignment

LEADING

The term **leading** refers to the space between the lines, but is measured from the baseline of one line to the baseline of the one below. Thus, the measurements quoted include the point size of the text itself.

Leading is a vital feature of text preparation. There is a standard leading of about $\frac{1}{5}$ of the point size of the text added on, in the majority of instances, automatically by the computer. Thus, 10 pt text has 12 pt leading, and 12 pt has 14 pt leading, and so on. However, there are very good reasons why a particular text block may need to have the setting changed.

In the first example, the leading is at the standard setting of $\frac{1}{5}$ more than the text height. This is a good readable setting. By comparison, the second example is difficult to read, as the leading has been reduced significantly. The leading in the last example has been increased to create an open easy-to-read effect and this technique is often used in magazines and newspapers, callouts and advertisements, where short pieces of text benefit from its use. There are examples in this book on pages 108 and 138.

Leading

Animals continue to enchant humans of all ages and all races. In the west we have endowed them with emotions and reactions that other races would not understand. There are species that have only been seen in films like armadillos and giant tortoises that have captured the imaginations of writers and animators to such an extent that whole industries have grown up around them. What about those films of prehistoric animals that seem real in snarl and bite and fright. They leap into life and have intents and instincts that we

Example 1 – 12 pt type on 14 pt leading

Animals continue to enchant humans of all ages and all races. In the west we have endowed them with emotions and reactions that other races would not understand. There are species that have only been seen in films like armadillos and giant tortoises that have captured the imaginations of writers and animators to such an extent that whole industries have grown up around them. What about those films of prehistoric animals that seem real in snarl and bite and fright. They leap into life and have intents and instincts that we have assumed our domestic pets have! Zoo keepers have stories of bringing up polar

Example 2 – 12 pt type on 12 pt leading

Animals continue to enchant humans of all ages and all races. In the west we have endowed them with emotions and reactions that other races would not understand. There are species that have only been seen in films like armadillos and giant tortoises that have captured the imaginations of writers and animators to such an extent that whole industries have grown up around them. What about those

Example 3 – 12 pt type on 18 pt leading

KERNING

This term refers to altering the space set by the desktop publishing package between letters. Some combinations of letters create an unattractively wide space between them, and you should reduce this space; other combinations leave the letters too close, and these should be made wider.

The space in real terms is very small; each adjustment is $\frac{1}{25}$ of an em space. **Kerning** concerns us most in larger point sizes, and especially in headlines and titles, between such combinations as are shown here. You will notice in the second sequence of combinations that the text is more attractive, as there are no distractions of extra or tight spaces.

Kerning

Before kerning

Wc WC Wd We William Wo Wq Wv
Ya YA Yc YC Ye Tc Te To Way

After kerning

Wc WC Wd We William Wo Wq Wv
Ya YA Yc YC Ye Tc Te To Way

Type the following four examples and kern them wherever necessary

The World Today

THE WORLD TODAY

Young Artists Yearbook

Families Check in Tomorrow

TRACKING

The space between characters can be adjusted by using the **tracking** facility. Generally, desktop publishers are advised to avoid changing the default tracking until they have gained extensive experience in dealing with typographical situations. As you can see in the examples here, the whole character of the text can be changed by selecting the options available. The only time tracking can be justifiably used, and then with caution, is to fit the last word of text within a specified column. Occasionally, it can be used to respace a heading where Force Justify is unsatisfactory.

Do not confuse kerning with tracking. To kern is to adjust the space between pairs of characters which are either noticeably too close or too far apart.

Apartments like these rarely come on the market. These have all been developed from a widely accepted formula that has sold well for the last four years but given individuality by being personalised for this site.

Example 1 – No tracking

Apartments like these rarely come on the market. These have all been developed from a widely accepted formula that has sold well for the last four years but given individuality by being personalised for this site.

Example 2 – Normal tracking

Tracking in justified text

Apartments like these rarely come on the market. These have all been developed from a widely accepted formula that has sold well for the last four years but given individuality by being personalised for this site.

Example 3 – Loose tracking

Apartments like these rarely come on the market. These have all been developed from a widely accepted formula that has sold well for the last four years but given individuality by being personalised for this site.

Example 4 – Very loose tracking

Apartments like these rarely come on the market. These have all been developed from a widely accepted formula that has sold well for the last four years but given individuality by being personalised for this site.

Example 5 – Tight tracking

Apartments like these rarely come on the market. These have all been developed from a widely accepted formula that has sold well for the last four years but given individuality by being personalised for this site.

Example 6 – Very tight tracking

TEXT WRAP AND STANDOFF

Text and images make their impact by careful and varied integration with each other. In the first example, the text is justified but is kept away from the frame around the illustration by setting a standoff of several points on the appropriate sides of the frame.

The second example shows how text must be arranged if the image is to be placed in the centre of a text block. Text cannot be read if it flows around the image on four sides. If the image straddles two columns, text will flow in a readable way and the image adds considerable interest to the layout of the information. See examples on page 114.

In the third example, the image has text closely following its outline but still not touching, as a standoff of 5 pts was set here. The effect was achieved by using the **manual textwrap** feature available on most packages, where you can integrate the text very cleverly and effectively.

Text wrap and standoff

Animals continue to enchant humans of all ages and all races. In the west we have endowed them with emotions and reactions that other races would not understand. There are species that have only been seen in films like armadillos and giant tortoises that have captured the imaginations of writers and animators to such an extent that whole industries have grown up around them. What

Example 1 – Frame with 2 mm standoff

Animals continue to enchant humans of all ages and all races. In the west we have endowed them with emotions and

reactions that other races would not understand. There are species that have only been seen in films like armadillos and giant tortoises that have captured What about those films of prehistoric

Example 2 – The only text flow for a central illustration

Animals continue to enchant humans of all ages and all races. In the west we have endowed them with emotions and reactions that other races would not understand. There are species that have only been seen in films like armadillos and giant tortoises that have capturedt h e imaginations of writers and animators to such an extent that whole industries have grown up around them. What about those films of prehistoric animals that seem real in snarl and bite and fright. They leap

Example 3 – Frame manually following image to allow close text flow

WIDOWS AND ORPHANS

These terms refer to undesirable lines of text that remain at the bottom of a column (an **orphan**), and at the top of a column (a **widow**). Every effort must be made to eliminate these lines. Various copy fitting techniques should be tried as outlined on pages 75 and 79 and, if all else fails, careful editing of the text should be done.

A widow

Widows and orphans

Animals continue to enchant humans of all ages and all races. In the west we have endowed them with emotions and reactions that other races would not understand.

There are species that have only been seen in films like armadillos and giant tortoises that have captured the imaginations of writers and animators to such an extent that whole industries have

grown up around them.

What about those films of prehistoric animals that seem real in snarl and bite and fright. They leap into life and have intents and instincts that we have assumed our domestic pets have!

Zoo keepers have stories of bringing up polar bears from birth and having to teach them how to be bears. And of course

Melanie was overjoyed at the prospect of visiting the prestigious Botanic Gardens in Collingsworth. Her work as a botanist had taken her there many years ago as a student but she had not been back. She knew how important an institution it had become in the conservation of wild species from the dry areas of India and Africa.

She even felt she had a claim

to some of its fame as she brought back several specimens as a student which convinced the Director at the time that there were genuses being wiped out without the indigenous population knowing.

Much of her work nowadays was involved with developing new strains with colours that would find popularity with the amateur gardener and in

An orphan

BULLETS

In these two exercises, we see how individual points can be made clearer by putting a simple eye-catching symbol at the start of the relevant line. These symbols are called **bullets**. There are a variety available, though it is often the simplest that are most effective.

Many desktop publishing packages have a Special Features option which includes bullets. Alternatively, the paragraph specifications allow you to select from a range of bullets with a size option as well.

If you do not have either of these facilities, you can create as wide a choice as any other method by using the Wingding font. As you can see in Appendix Three, the Wingding font is just a series of symbols.

Place, for instance, a lower case **n** before the paragraph you wish to bullet, select the Wingding font, having highlighted that character, and it becomes the symbol shown in the following example. Prepare this sample as shown and then experiment with other lower-case characters, to become familiar with what is available. Another technique is to create the bullet and then copy it to be pasted into subsequent positions.

NOTES ON THE FOLLOWING EXERCISES

    a. The point size of the bullet was increased to be significant next to the text.

    b. To ensure that the bullet rests at the x-height, the **baseline shift** was used on the selected bullet and shifted down.

Bullets
Example 1

> ## Our clients enjoy several things about this agency and the survey shows:
>
> ◼   The fast turnaround satisfied 90% of the clients since January.
>
> ◼   Our expertise in colour and artwork was warmly praised by nearly all the respondents.
>
> ◼   The breakdown of charges shown on our clients' invoices enables them to make exact costings for future jobs.

THESE ITEMS ARE ESSENTIAL

- Waterproof outer wear

- Two pairs of walking boots

- A complete change of underwear

- A comprehensive first aid kit

Bullets
Example 2

COPY AND PASTE, MULTIPLE PASTE, CUT AND PASTE

The copy and paste routine is one of the most useful features of desktop publishing. A selected object is cut or copied to the clipboard, which is an unseen portion of the computer's memory. The examples on page 66 show that text, images and graphics can all be cut and pasted. In example 1, an image has been imported once and carefully placed. By marking it and selecting **Copy** and then selecting **Paste**, the image can be reproduced. You need to repeat the paste selection for the number of times you want to reproduce the item, if your package does not have a multiple paste feature. This feature enables you to determine how many copies you wish to have and where in relation to each other you want them to appear. Remember that the clipboard is only available for one copy at a time and so, whenever you copy another item to it, the previous one is removed.

Cut and **Paste** is used when an item is to be removed from its present position and then pasted into another. In this case, too, **Multiple Paste** is effective. **Clear** means exactly that — the item is gone for good.

It is worth remembering to transform your item before you copy and paste it, as it is difficult to get several copies exactly the same after pasting. For example, the first sprig of flowers was rotated to the right, the second was rotated to the left, and both were pasted for the last two images. It would have been complicated to get them symmetrical after pasting.

*Copy and paste
and multiple paste*

DREAMS ARE
AN IMPORTANT
PART OF
REALITY

DREAMS ARE
AN IMPORTANT
PART OF
REALITY

DREAMS ARE
AN IMPORTANT
PART OF
REALITY

Example 1 – Text copied twice

*Example 2 – Image and frame
copied twice*

*Example 3 – An image copied
once only after transformation*

SEND TO BACK AND TO FRONT

Documents which consist of several elements can be difficult to control, unless the **Send to Back** and **Bring to Front** commands are used. The first element can get lost behind the next one created, or imported and positioned. As the piece develops, you can select the most recent element and continuously bring it to the front, but this may put other elements out of order.

One solution is to create all the elements separately on the pasteboard and position them together roughly. Then select the one required at the front first and send it to the back, select the one required behind that and send it to the back, and treat the other elements similarly. This way you end up with the items stacked in the correct order.

From the example here, you would develop each of the four parts and, accepting the initial disorder when you assemble them, correct it by selecting the text first to go to back, then the image, then the inner frame and lastly the tinted rectangle which should now have a line of none. Follow the example here to test out the procedure.

Send to back and to front

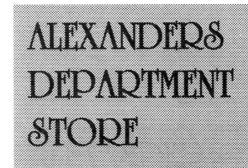

Created first

Created second with 20% tints and line to none

Another section, the image, retrieved

The final component, the inner frame, drawn but assembled in the stacking order

REVERSED TEXT ON TINTED FIELDS

This is used to add emphasis and interest to headings and main points. First, create a tinted frame (often it is worth keeping to low densities and finally making them 100%). On this frame, type the text and, having highlighted the text, choose **Reversed** or **Reversed Out** from Text Styles. The normally black characters will be white but hidden in the black of the highlight. Click off the highlight to see the white text and, finally, make the frame completely black if you want a very contrasting effect. Work the examples shown here for practice. In the fourth example, the central circle was given a fill of paper, which appears very white against the rectangular tint because **Paper** indicates a blank area which covers up anything beneath it. This is different from the fill of **Transparent**, where items which lie within its area are visible.

Reversed text

Example 1 – 80% fill

Example 2 – 40% fill

Example 3 – 30% fill

Example 4 – Mixed fills with a circle of 'paper'

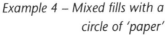

CROPPING

This term refers to taking away part of an image, by **cropping**, to leave the required section. There is usually a tool in the toolbox especially for this function. When the image has been cropped, it is frequently required to be stretched as well, to fit the space and still maintain its aspect ratio. The effects of these manoeuvres can be seen in examples 1 – 4 below.

In the second half of the page, small copies have been placed while others have been copied and then reflected on a vertical axis at 180 degrees.

The very bottom of the page shows a small section retained from the original image, copied, reflected and now awaiting further parts or additions from a paint program to make a completely new creature!

Using images offers us the opportunity to be creative, even if they are taken from a library of clip art. Often they can be used just as they are or changed within the DTP program by cropping. Imaginative cropping can produce a whole new picture, and parts retained can be cut and pasted to make further patterns.

In the first instance, practise cropping the image to leave about two thirds and then, following examples here, try out your own ideas on images you may have that came with your package or which are on the accompanying disk.

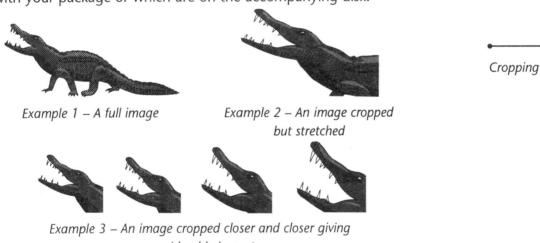

Cropping

Example 1 – A full image　　　*Example 2 – An image cropped but stretched*

Example 3 – An image cropped closer and closer giving considerable impact

this section has been cropped

Example 4 – Part of the head cropped, rotated and mirrored to create a different idea completely

ASPECT RATIO

In some situations, images are imported into a desktop publishing document in their saved state. However, images are often required for a space which is of different dimensions from the original illustration. Usually, the original **aspect ratio**, which is the relation of height to width (a ratio of 1:1), is maintained — in some packages by restraining the import by keeping the shift key down. It is better to have white space around a picture within its given space than fill the space and have an image distorted by squeezing up the picture (example 2) or stretching it to fit! On the other hand, some interesting effects can be achieved by using the **stretch** feature, as we can see in example 4.

Combining stretching with cropping enables us to use one image in an article but present it in several different ways to have interest and emphasis throughout. The techniques of cropping, stretching, mirroring and rotating have all been combined in example 4 on page 69, where a small part of the alligator's head has been used to form the basis of another animal entirely.The 'family of alligators', example 5 on page 71, illustrates maintaining the aspect ratio in very much smaller sizes while these images are being mirrored or flipped. The nearest one on the left has been slightly rotated as well.

Maintaining aspect ratio and the effects of distortion

Example 1 – An image with accurate aspect ratio

Example 2 – An image with distorted aspect ratio

Example 3 – A cropped image with the aspect ratio maintained

Example 4 – A cropped image with the aspect ratio effectively distorted

Example 5 – Images retaining the aspect ratio but made smaller (and two mirrored)

ROTATING, SKEWING AND MIRRORING

These transformations are easily achieved in nearly all desktop publishing packages. The term to **skew** means that the image is moved on an axis in a particular direction with some distortion. In example 2, we see the clothes horse skewed clockwise 30 degrees (while to skew anti-clockwise is indicated by a minus in the selection box). An image is said to be **rotated** when it is completely turned about a central point, as in example 4 where 45 degrees and 90 degrees are illustrated.

The **mirroring** (or **flipping**) transformation offers two possibilities — **vertical** and **horizontal**. In example 6 – 7, the giraffe is first imported facing right, copied and then mirrored to face left, which is a vertical transformation. Some images lend themselves to mirroring horizontally (usually in pattern making) and example 8 illustrates well the **horizontal mirror** by its dramatic effect. It should be used with discretion!

Rotating, skewing and mirroring

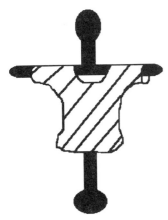

Example 1 – The original image

Example 2 – The original image skewed 30°

Example 3 – The original image skewed -30°

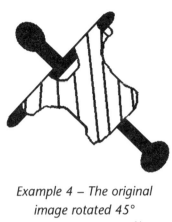

*Example 4 – The original
image rotated 45°*

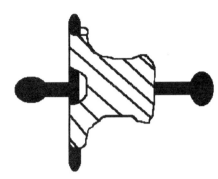

*Example 5 – The original
image rotated 90°*

*Example 6-7 – The original image placed, copied and then
mirrored vertically*

*Example 8 – The original
image mirrored
horizontally and vertically!*

PIXEL EDITING

Some examining bodies (the City and Guilds of London is one) require candidates to edit an image at the **pixel** level. This requirement is to ensure that students learn what makes up an image on the screen, as well as introducing them to the fundamentals of editing. Your paint program will enable you to **Zoom In** to the image so that a small section is enlarged. You will have to identify the area to be edited first and then, using the mouse, turn on (make black or coloured) with the left mouse button or turn off using the right mouse button (make white) those pixels which will alter the image. Zooming into images enables a clean-up operation to be done on scanned images, which often pick up greyness or 'noise' which is detected by the laser beam of the scanner.

The images below should be loaded into your paint program from the accompanying disk and edited as shown. Precision is of the essence here, so zoom in as closely as possible. Remember to save the changed image with another file name, so that the original is still intact.

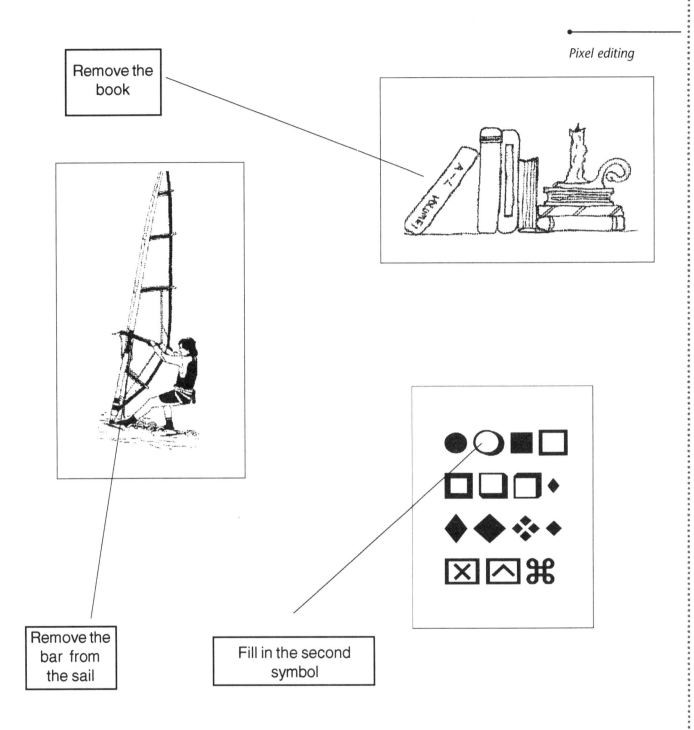

Pixel editing

Remove the book

Remove the bar from the sail

Fill in the second symbol

EXPORTING TEXT

As a general rule, you will import text of more than a few lines into your desktop publishing document from your word processing program, but there are times when you type text in and within a short while there is a considerable amount of text on screen. On other occasions, you may import text and edit it, but in so doing make considerable changes to the text.

In both cases, it may be necessary to have an accurate file of the text saved separately as an ASCII file. It would be tedious to return to the original or retype the input text. Instead, desktop publishing programs provide an **export** facility. Once the text to be saved is marked, usually with the I-beam, it can be exported via the File menu to the directory where all your desktop publishing text is kept. It is saved only as an ASCII file.

GRIDS

As soon as you progress in this course to columnar work, you should prepare the exercises before you go to the computer. The overall design should be established by drawing out a sketch of the finished document, showing the approximate positions of headlines, text, images and graphic lines. Professional designers start with a **grid**, on which they indicate the elements of their document. This grid is then transferred to the electronic page by using guide lines and column indicators. Typical grids are shown below (in fact the right-hand one is of exercise 37).

Grids

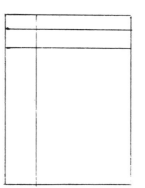
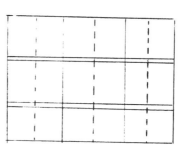

· PART THREE ·

EXAMINATION PREPARATION AND BEYOND

These first three exercises are exact requirements from City and Guilds (Assignments Level I) examination questions.

▼ EXERCISE 20

TWO COLUMNS

At Page Setup select A4 portrait with 20 mm margins left, right and top, and with 25 mm at the bottom. There are to be two columns. There is a 1 pt graphic line in the gutter. Import the text supplied (Techno.txt). Use the headline and subhead provided.

The headline is serif, 36 pts, bold and centred.

The body text is to be serif, 12 pts on 14 pt leading, and justified. Divide into suitable paragraphs. This example has 3 mm space after the paragraphs rather than another blank line entered.

Subheads are sans serif, 14 pts on 18 pt leading, left aligned, and bold.

Meeting the above specifications is straightforward, but copy fitting is a considerable feature of this exercise as well. The best technique is to work on the document as a whole, getting all the elements reasonably right and, if possible, print out a draft copy* from which to make adjustments.

You should identify the areas where there is room for manoeuvre. Here are some guidelines.

The headline could be moved slightly up or down, the subhead could have a 1 mm space after added or the 'space after' could be adjusted so that the two columns end at exactly the same horizontal point. **Save As** futpar.???. **Print** one copy.

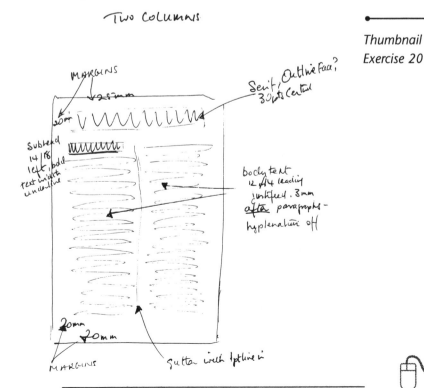

Thumbnail Exercise 20

*This facility is not available under examination conditions.

Two columns

THE COMMUNICATIONS JOURNAL

WORKING PRACTICES FOR THE FUTURE

Anyone entering an administrative environment should be fully conversant with what is called Office Technology. Each component of this matrix has an individual part to play in communications as well as being a vital link in the chain of faster more efficient data exchange.

We can see from the widespread use of Word Processing that computerisation has become the essential tool for administrative information gathering, output, and recording. The integrated office system has been with us now for long enough for what used to be the slow interaction between one software package and another to take place on screen and almost simultaneously. Data can be captured, stored, retrieved and reused in an entirely different package within seconds and by the same user. End users are increasingly imaginative with the use of the integrated package and develop personal routes and shortcuts to the desired objective.

The stand alone PC was eagerly accepted by many and abhorred by just as many employees. Just around the corner was the Network! This has called for a new attitude to work practices and what can be described as ownership of a project or part of it. Users may indeed be responsible for a particular part of, say, the design of a building, but interaction with others doing their part may be very limited, and involvement in the finished product when bringing it all together may not take place. Job satisfaction has to come from other areas than the finished design.

The network has placed the responsibility for the technical integrity of the system in the hands of an expert who may or may not work in a hands-on role on the project. Some users are much happier knowing that specialist help is on hand when problems to do with the system occur; however, some would like to deal with a network manager who understands the needs of users and the priorities they have in their work as well as the high standards they wish to reach.

Telecommunications advancements have impinged on all administrative staff. Not only have we seen an exceptional explosion in Telesales recently but there is an expectation that all employees will be conversant with Data bases provided by the country's Television and Telecommunications service. So many companies rely on up to the minute information on currencies, credit ratings, sales figures, trends in markets, movement of goods and money that employees are expected to be able to retrieve this data from whatever source the company is linked to. Some businesses stand or fall just on the strengths of their computerised systems and their network capabilites, the travel industry for instance.

In this case we cannot imagine a successful venture unless mobile phones, fax machines, photocopiers, modems and computers work in tandem to provide the proprietor and their clients with communications facilities of the highest order.

Networks and telecommunications have brought widely spread organisations together in a way that ignores time and space differences. Local networks linked to others and linked via bridges to wider networks means that data captured in one location can be available in another part of the world and acted upon within minutes.

We may work more closely with people on other networks than with the people in the same building. This raises questions about the value we place on human interaction and increased preciousness of face to face communication and personal relationships. Schools and parents should be aware of how different the world young people will be working in is from the one they went into and what limited chances there are in some jobs for people to be themselves.

▼ EXERCISE 21

THREE PARAGRAPHS WITH SUBHEADINGS

(This exercise is direct preparation for an assignment set by the City and Guilds, Level I.)

New features

1   **selecting lines under text as part of the text style**

2   **re-assembling text into larger sections**

3   **adjusting the position of all elements on a page to achieve copy fitting**

For this **New** document, select even margins of 20 mm all round.

Input the following as a heading — 30 pts, centred, and serif font.

TECHNOLOGY TODAY

Import the text Techno.txt for the body text.

Re-assemble the text into three fairly equal blocks. Before the first section, input this subheading

DATA EXCHANGE

Before the second section, input this subheading

THE PERSONAL COMPUTER

Before the third section, input this subheading

DATABASE USES

For these subheads, select a sans serif font of 14 pts on 18 pt leading, left aligned with a 1 pt line selected as part of the type style. This is often found in the Paragraph dialog box under Rules. At the same time, select a 3 mm space below this rule.

Body text is serif, 12 pts on 14 pt leading and justified.

Some copy fitting will have to be done at this stage. Use the recommended methods in the previous exercise. You are expected to get the text on the page with no visible distortion to the measurements given. Draw a 1 pt line below the text, on the bottom margin. Beneath this, put your name and college address. **Save As** 3partec.??? and **Print** one copy.

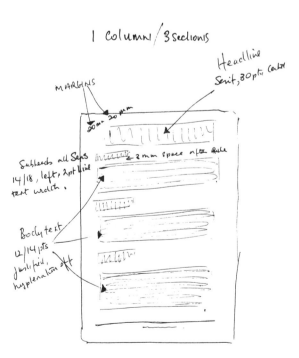

Thumbnail Exercise 21

TECHNOLOGY TODAY

DATA EXCHANGE

Anyone entering an administrative environment should be fully conversant with what is called Office Technology. Each component of this matrix has an individual part to play in communications as well as being a vital link in the chain of faster more efficient data exchange. We can see from the widespread use of Word Processing that computerisation has become the essential tool for administrative information gathering, output, and recording. The integrated office system has been with us now for long enough for what used to be the slow interaction between one software package and another to take place on screen and almost simultaneously. Data can be captured, stored, retrieved and reused in an entirely different package within seconds and by the same user. End users are increasingly imaginative with the use of the integrated package and develop personal routes and shortcuts to the desired objective.

THE PERSONAL COMPUTER

The stand alone PC was eagerly accepted by many and abhorred by just as many employees. Just around the corner was the Network! This has called for a new attitude to work practices and what can be described as ownership of a project or part of it. Users may indeed be responsible for a particular part of, say, the design of a building, but interaction with others doing their part may be very limited, and involvement in the finished product when bringing it all together may not take place. Job satisfaction has to come from other areas than the finished design. The network has placed the responsibility for the technical integrity of the system in the hands of an expert who may or may not work in a hands-on role on the project. Some users are much happier knowing that specialist help is on hand when problems to do with the system occur; however, some would like to deal with a network manager who understands the needs of users and the priorities they have in their work as well as the high standards they wish to reach.

DATABASE USES

Telecommunications advancements have impinged on all administrative staff. Not only have we seen an exceptional explosion in Telesales recently but there is an expectation that all employees will be conversant with Data bases provided by the country's Television and Telecommunications service. So many companies rely on up to the minute information on currencies, credit ratings, sales figures, trends in markets, movement of goods and money that employees are expected to be able to retrieve this data from whatever source the company is linked to. Some businesses stand or fall just on the strengths of their computerised systems and their network capabilites, the travel industry for instance. In this case we cannot imagine a successful venture unless mobile phones, fax machines, photocopiers, modems and computers work in tandem to provide the proprietor and their clients with communications facilities of the highest order. Networks and telecommunications have brought widely spread organisations together in a way that ignores time and space differences. Local networks linked to others and linked via bridges to wider networks means that data captured in one location can be available in another part of the world and acted upon within minutes. We may work more closely with people on other networks than with the people in the same building. This raises questions about the value we place on human interaction and increased preciousness of face to face communication and personal relationships. Schools and parents should be aware of how different the world young people will be working is in from the one they went into and what limited chances there are in some jobs for people to be themselves.

Student name and College etc

▼ EXERCISE 22

THREE COLUMNS

On a single page, set up the following.

Margins of 25 mm top and 20 mm left, right and bottom.

Three columns with 5 mm gutters.

1 pt graphic line drawn from margin to margin across the bottom of the page.

The text specifications are:

Headline is 30 pts, serif, centred, bold.

The body text is serif, 12 on 14 pt leading, left aligned, with hyphenation on.

Subheadings are sans serif, 14 on 18 pt leading, left, bold, with a .5 pt line as part of the text.

Input the headline.

Import the text Techno.txt, flowing it into the three columns. Divide it into three reasonably equal sections. Each is to be preceded by a subheading (Data exchange, workstations, Databases).

In this exercise, hyphenation has been used to make the best use of the narrow column width.

Although the last three points cover the essentials of this assignment, there are two major improvements you can make to add professionalism to the document.

1. Copy fit carefully so that the text begins and ends at the same point in each column. You can adjust the paragraph breaks with the addition of .5 mm, or adjust the tracking (see page 61) in a section. If these options do not solve the problem, you could edit the text with extreme care.
2. Kern the headline, especially between the CH, OLO, GY, DA and AY.

Save As 3coltec.??? and **Print** one copy.

Thumbnail
Exercise 22

THREE COLUMNS

MARGIN TOP
25

left
20

Serif
30pts
centred

gutter 5mm

Subheads 14/18 leading
Sans Serif
left, bold
line 12u width

MARGIN
20 mm

body Text Serif
12/14 leading
Justified
Hyphenation off

MARGINS

Gutters 5mm

TECHNOLOGY TODAY

DATA EXCHANGE

Anyone entering an administrative environment should be fully conversant with what is called Office Technology. Each component of this matrix has an individual part to play in communications as well as being a vital link in the chain of faster more efficient data exchange. We can see from the widespread use of Word Processing that computerisation has become the essential tool for administrative information gathering, output, and recording. The integrated office system has been with us now for long enough for what used to be the slow interaction between one software package and another to take place on screen and almost simultaneously. Data can be captured, stored, retrieved and reused in an entirely different package within seconds and by the same user. End users are increasingly imaginative with the use of the integrated package and develop personal routes and shortcuts to the desired objective.

WORKSTATIONS

The stand alone PC was eagerly accepted by many and abhorred by just as many employees. Just around the corner was the Network! This has called for a new attitude to work practices and what can be described as ownership of a project or part of it. Users may indeed be responsible for a particular part of, say, the design of a building, but interaction with others doing their part may be very limited, and involvement in the finished product when bringing it all together may not take place.

Job satisfaction has to come from other areas than the finished design. The network has placed the responsibility for the technical integrity of the system in the hands of an expert who may or may not work in a hands-on role on the project. Some users are much happier knowing that specialist help is on hand when problems to do with the system occur; however, some would like to deal with a network manager who understands the needs of users and the priorities they have in their work load.

Telecommunications advancements have impinged on all administrative staff. Not only have we seen an exceptional explosion in Telesales recently but there is an expectation that all employees will be conversant with Data bases provided by the country's Television and Telecommunications service. So many companies rely on up to the minute information on currencies, credit ratings, sales figures, trends in markets, movement of goods and money that employees are expected to be able to retrieve this data from whatever source the company is linked to. Some businesses stand or fall just on the strengths of their computerised systems and their network capabilites, the travel industry for instance.

In this case we cannot imagine a successful venture unless mobile phones, fax machines, photocopiers, modems and computers work in tandem to provide the proprietor and their clients with communications facilities of the highest order. Networks and telecommunication have brought widely spread organisations together in a way that ignores time and space differences.

DATABASES

Local networks linked to others and linked via bridges to wider networks means that data captured in one location can be available in another part of the world and acted upon within minutes. he social implications of these recent changes are wide indeed. As users and employees we can be forgiven at times if we are wary of interaction with people we are not face to face with. We may not be interacting with another person on the phone when voice recognition becomes more widely available. We may be booking our tickets for theatres and trains with pre-recorded voices which can interpret our requests and send out our order immediately. We may work more closely with people on other networks than with the people in the same building. This raises questions about the value we place on human interaction and increased preciousness of face to face communication and personal relationships. Schools and parents should be aware of how different the world young people will be working in is from the one they went into and what limited chances there are in some employment for people to be themselves.

▼ EXERCISE 23
PROOF CORRECTION MARKS

Frequently, as a desktop publisher, you will receive text matter that has been proofread and now has to be corrected. Professional proofreaders use correction marks that are understood by everyone dealing with text.

The two examples that follow use the most commonly encountered marks. These and others in frequent use are listed in Appendix Five. You should type the corrected versions into a word processing program, saving them as ASCII files: 'Rural Industrialisation' as Rural.??? and 'The Lost Opportunity' as Lostop.???. They are to be used in the following two exercises.

Text for correction 1

Rural Industrialisation   Capitals

3 They had booked in May for this holiday, full of expectation that at last   indent
they would meet the friends and family they had only heard about till now.
Getting to Beauvais had not been difficult, in fact the good weather and   ,
roads and meant an earlier arrival than either of them had expected.   ∂

Sylvia had left the grey atmosphere of manchester knowing John was   capital
driving down from Glasgow that morning too so they could leave together   ∂
from Victoria Station. They had talked often about his brother Stephen   trs
who had settled in FRANCE to set up his own business in prepacked   ≢
gourmet foods. He had become extremely successful, employing ten at
first and now twenty-one cooks, packers and distributors. Sylvia had   New para
worked out that Stephen must have made enough money already to buy
significant property in the nearby town of Merrior. perhaps that's the   Cap
reason he has for never coming back home. Too busy, too expensive and
he loved Merrior!   embolden

Driving through the rich pasture lands of France Sylvia and John were
silent. Occasionally they needed to consult the map/The peacefulness was   ⊙
affecting them - there was no hurry, no timetable and no one had   ,
expectations. However, they did want to know more about Stephens   ⸮
business and the few close friends he had made during the last five years.

Text for correction 2

[THE LOST OPPORTUNITY?]   Centre

"Wait/she said as the door closed behind her. She could see Jason just
leaving by the main revolving door. If she lost sight of him now she'd
never catch up with him and be able to continue the banter they had started
late that afternoon.   No new paragraph

efficient

He had always seemed so organised and effecient. And now some aspects   ∂ capital
of him seemed just ordinary and quite likeable. To see him making simple
mistakes at the meeting and laughing about it afterwards completely
changed her impression of him. She had read the Internal Promotions   New para
notices and when the Assistant Design Director position was advertised
she knew that was a job she should be applying for. Jason's cold and at
times unhelpful manner had been the reason for delaying her application.
Maybe now she could see herself working well in that department. The
only problem was could he!

The workload in the design department was onerous. Every morning   capital
Someone was in early planning layouts and alternatives that clients might
prefer even though several had already been set up. Generally six projects
could be handled at once and each one of them developed their own
workstyle without intruding too much on each/other.

PASSAGE 1

Rural Industrialisation

This passage is the beginning of a short story due to be published in a magazine. It has been sent to you, firstly to correct and save and then to consider its use in the overall design of the magazine page. You should create a sketch, showing how this text and the continuing text will be placed on the page, as well as the type style and size for the title, by line, and position of any illustrations you wish to include. You would get some ideas by consulting magazines, especially the start pages of articles and short stories where the combination of images and text sets the tone of the whole text.

PASSAGE 2

The Lost Opportunity

The second passage is the start of a chapter in a romantic story. You are to design this page by first creating a sketch showing the position of the text, margins, any embellishments like chapter numbering, drop caps, graduated text sizes and body text specifications. Use your corrected text to create this mock-up.

▼ EXERCISE 24
ERRATA SLIP

This document is a small information sheet that is sometimes found in publications like programmes and books, when data has changed after printing.

At **New** and **Custom,** set up these dimensions: 105 mm wide x 75 mm deep and margins of 10 mm all round. The dashed frame here need not appear on your printout; it is used to define the area in which to place the text. Attend carefully to the changes in size and style of the text. In this example, the type sizes are between 12 and 10 pts only. **Save As** errata.??? and **Print** one copy with printer's marks.

A8 with appropriate type size and style

ERRATA SLIP

THE PUBLISHERS WISH TO ADVISE READERS OF THESE ERRORS UNDETECTED AT THE TIME OF GOING TO PRESS:

1 Page 31
The paragraph beginning *"Terminals with digitisers ..."* and ending with *"...are at the forefront of modern development."* should be omitted.
2 Page 40
The captions a) and b) should be reversed.

FOLLOW-UP EXERCISE

Using the same page size, prepare the text for the following situation.

Employers are enclosing with payslips a notice to the effect that employees who have been with the company for over 5 years are due two days' extra holiday this year.

Employees with 6 months to 5 years are due one day. **Save As** holerata.???. **Print** one copy without printer's marks.

▼ EXERCISE 25

MAGAZINE COVER — USING TYPEFACES IMAGINATIVELY

In this exercise you will have the opportunity to explore the typefaces available on your system.

In this example, a point size of 108 was used for all but the last line, where 90 pts was used to keep the word on one line.

Notice that upper and lower case letters have been combined with italic and bold. The usual leading here has been abandoned, to place the individual characters close enough to show any pattern in the choice of font and make the overall effect concentrated. The **ampersand** has been placed so as to indicate that it is in its own space. It is usual, when using a variety of typefaces in this way, to indicate by their use the areas to which the output refers. For example, a design may have to do with sport, and great play can be made of the characters because of this.

You can obtain very interesting effects with very few fonts — the technique is in combining upper and lower case with emboldening, italics and a variety of leading that is different from the standard, as well as intensive kerning.

As a start, you may wish to copy this example. Here are some suggestions you could follow up, using whatever fonts you have to help convey originality in the text and the idea behind it.

Design typographical features for the following

1. a label for a jar of Curry Sauce

2. a ticket for an exhibition game of basketball

3. a label attached to furniture about flame resistance

A variety of typefaces

The Specialist Magazone for Desktop Publishers   January 1996

Typo Graphy & Today Tomorrow

Published by Hargreaves and McHugh   London and New York

▼ EXERCISE 26

A HOLIDAY ENQUIRY FORM — USING THE TABULAR STOP

This form is basically in three columns, but not of equal width. The column width is established by the details that will be filled in on the form, rather than meeting strict requirements for equal proportions. For example, the first two items will obviously take up more character space than the telephone number. After that, the text input here was set up to follow the horizontal position of the first section where possible. The tab stop was used to move across the page for the text at the default tab distance.

Three type styles were created, apart from the main heading. A serif text of 14 pts was used throughout, while the 'official' section has 16 pts serif with underline as part of the paragraph characteristics just text wide. The small text is 12 pts. Two widths of graphic line were used, .5 pt for the fill-ins and 2 pts for the dividing line. The first was copied and pasted, using the side ruler to place them (in a very close view) exactly 10 mm apart. Two fills were used to highlight the most relevant sections for the travel agent. The filled rectangles here have a line set to none. **Save As** Holform.???. **Print** one copy and choose 85% scaling to 'tighten up' the finished form.

This form could well become the basis for others that any organisation may need. So keeping the blank as a master to be adapted as needs arose would save a lot of time.

Thumbnail
Exercise 26

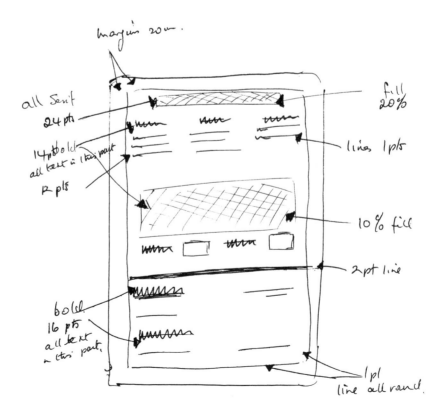

HOLIDAY ENQUIRY FORM

NAME   **ADDRESS**   **TELEPHONE**

       Work _____

Title _____   Home _____

First Name _____

Surname _____

HOLIDAY NO _____   **BROCHURE DATE** _____

DESTINATION 1st preference _____ **DATE** _____

2nd preference _____ **DATE** _____

HOTEL ☐   **APARTMENT** ☐

NO OF TRAVELLERS Adults _____ Children _____

SPECIAL REQUESTS _____

_____

OFFICIAL USE ONLY

AGENTS NO _____   Telephone No _____

       Extn _____

Follow up

Telesales Rep No _____   Final response _____

▼ EXERCISE 27

BUSINESS STATIONERY — LETTERHEAD, BUSINESS CARD AND COMPLIMENT SLIP

LETTERHEAD

Using A4 portrait, set margins of 20 mm left and right, 15 mm top and bottom. The finished letterhead should end 70 mm down from the top of the page.

Text like this is best input with each item as a separate paragraph with its own text box, for easier manoeuvrability.

Input the following

Paragon Packaging

203 Merlyn Industrial Estate

Dublin 24

Tel 242476

It is important at this stage to set up the type specification, so that, for the next two assignments, only the type sizes and alignment need to be changed. The font stays the same, to keep consistency within the house style.

Import the logo you created earlier in the course (exercise 17), saved as Logo.???, and reduce its size to fit, as indicated. Remember, if you are using desktop publishing under Windows, you can copy and paste from one page, document and package to another. Once you have the letterhead set out, you can paste the logo into the compliment slip and into the business card.

Letterhead

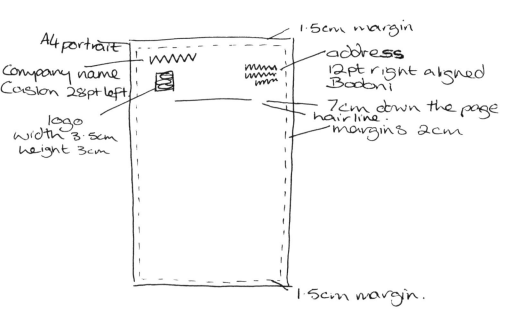

A4 portrait
Company name
Caslon 28pt left
logo
width 3.5cm
height 3cm

1.5cm margin
address
12pt right aligned
Bodoni
7cm down the page
hairline.
margins 2cm

1.5cm margin.

COMPLIMENT SLIP

Select A4 with 15 mm margins. Compliment slips are designed to use only one third of an A4 sheet, so that they will fit into the standard A4 envelope, as well as to keep the space for the message to a reasonable but small area.

In the top 100 mm of the A4, the same details can be copied and pasted from the letterhead, changing the alignment and size as shown below. The new detail to be typed in is

With Compliments

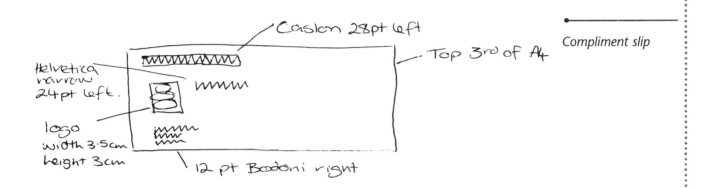

Compliment slip

BUSINESS CARD

At **New,** select **custom** and **landscape** for the business card. The dimensions are 90 mm wide and 60 mm deep.* It is not necessary to show the hairline frame in your printout — it is shown here so that the screen area is defined.

The text is the same that was used in the exercise for the letterhead. The only new line of text to insert here is

MONICA MALLOY Designer

The type specs are shown in the diagram below. You should import the logo you created earlier in the course as Logo.??? and reduce its size to fit this small area as well as leave sufficient white space to set off all the details. **Save As** Buscd.???.

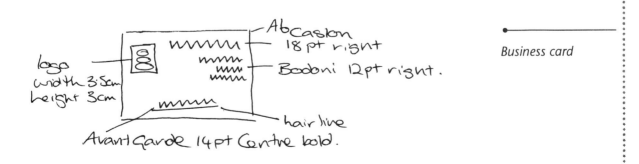

Business card

---

*The dimensions quoted here are those specified in the City and Guilds Level II syllabus. However, the standard measurements in use for a business card are 80 x 50 mm, and this is the area you should work on in subsequent exercises, reducing the type size accordingly.

SUPPLEMENTARY EXERCISE

In Appendix Seven you will find several logos that can be used in the same way as the one you have created.

Use the footnote dimensions to develop a letterhead, compliment slip and business card along similar lines, using the Warick Medical Suppliers logo. The job title is Senior Sales Representative. Use your own name, and devise an address for the company. This assignment links with the acetates in exercise 46, giving a wider house style application.

There are also logos for carpentry and building enterprises that you can use in the same way, or use paint and design programs to develop your own logos. Remember, too, that a business card can look very attractive in portrait orientation.

Paragon Packaging

203 Merlyn Industrial Estate
Dublin 24
Tel 242476

Paragon Packaging

With Compliments

203 Merlyn Industrial Estate
Dublin 24
Tel 242476

Paragon Packaging

203 Merlyn Industrial Estate
Dublin 24
Tel 242476

MONICA MALLOY Designer

▼ EXERCISE 28
ROTATED TEXT

In the following exercise there are two typical examples of how rotated text is used. Frequently, photographs are credited with very small type at the side of the image, and attention-seeking headlines can be rotated.

For this exercise, on A4 prepare a rectangle 50 mm x 60 mm with a double line. Insert the caption in a small italic type style. Use a similar typeface for the photograph credit. Use the rotate tool to place this within a millimetre of the frame. The rotated headline is at 35 degrees, in serif, 18 pts and centred within its text box.

The descriptive paragraphs are in 14 pt Times New Roman, with left alignment. Feel free to develop this exercise by enhancing the paragraphs with drop capitals, wider leading or any other acceptable enhancements.

The image in the frame was created in a paint program, then copied and pasted via the clipboard into the desktop publishing document. It could also be made in a drawing package, grouped and taken as a unit via the clipboard, or saved as an image and imported formally into the document. You may be able to do all this in your desktop publishing program, sizing it to fit the frame on completing the group routine. The image is available on the disk provided.

*Thumbnail
Exercise 28*

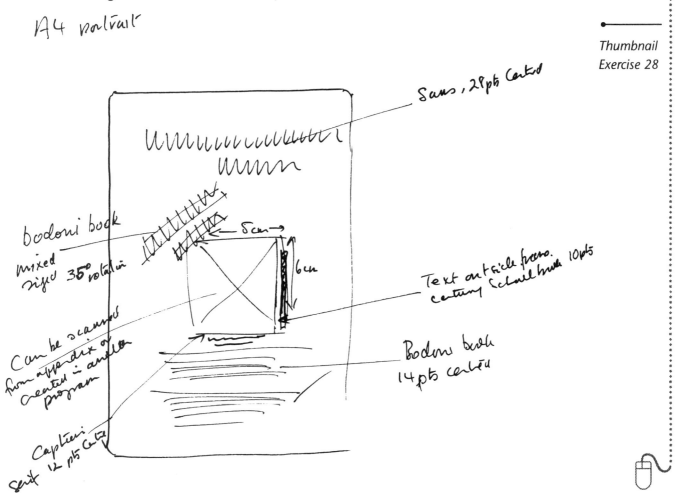

AWARD WINNING CEREMONIES OF THE DESIGN WORLD

FIFTH ANNUAL CONFERENCE OF STUDENT DESIGNERS

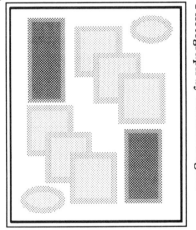

Photograph by Jordan Hughes

Jeanie Harris' winning design '96

This year we are fortunate in having the most publicised designers from the **European** Student circuit. ***Mark Ellis*** and ***Helen Croxley*** are working with our own entrants to ensure they have the most up-to-date and eye catching designs from which to create their entries.

You are invited to attend the finals of this event on production of the card attached. Seat numbers are allocated strictly in accordance with the numbers shown on the card.

▼ EXERCISE 29

TWO A5 ADVERTISEMENTS, PRINTED WITH CROP MARKS

TELECOMMUNICATIONS OPEN WEEKEND

At **New**, select A5 portrait, 5 mm margins left and right and 15 mm margins top and bottom. All the text is centred, with a variety of typefaces and sizes and careful use of emboldening. You should experiment with the fonts available in your package to achieve a similar effect to the example. Save as Telecom.???. **Print**, selecting **Printer's Marks** (or crop marks) to produce the lines which indicate the exact limit of the pages.

MARKET GARDEN

Exactly the same setup is used for this advertisement. The alignment is more varied and the inclusion of an off-centre image makes it more interesting. Note also how the fruit extending beyond the frame adds impact. **Save As** Market.???. Remember to select **Printer's Marks** when you print.

*Thumbnail
Exercise 29*

A5 ADVERTISEMENTS TELECOMMUNICATIONS

MARKET GARDEN

A5 advertisements with crop marks

FILBURTON
TELECOMMUNICATIONS STATION

OPEN WEEKEND

May 18 - 19 1996

Lectures, Tours, Videos and Exhibitions

STUDENTS WELCOME ON
SATURDAY 18th
to use our Library facilities and
hear Dr R J Heinl deliver the
1996 Gowan Lecture

NO ADMISSION CHARGE

MARKET GARDEN

Every Saturday and Sunday at Glenhaven Hall

Specialists in Horticulture

Vegetables
Shrubs
Fruit Trees
Bedding Plants

Growers will be there to advise you.
No better value for the amateur gardener
who wants to get professional results!

▼ EXERCISE 30
STYLE SHEETS (MASTER PAGES OR TEMPLATES)

The following exercise requires the use of a **style sheet**, **template** or **master page**. Your program will use one of these definitions. Style sheets are used to set up specifications for material that is required many times and is to be presented in the same format. Style sheets contain details about margins, headers, footers, page numbers and graphics that are required, either from page to page in a multi-page document, or on a repeating basis over time.

Desktop publishing packages vary slightly in the way master sheets are set up and saved. Many applications come with a library of master sheets, which you can adapt to your requirements and save again under another name, preserving the original for further adaptation or use as it stands. Usually these are in a subdirectory of their own, and it would be wise for you to keep yours in a file for style sheets.

Check to see what the extension is, if it is not put in automatically on saving. Make sure you give it a name that links it in your mind with the graphics, text, and document name, for easy assembly at any time.

You are likely to find an icon representing the **Style Sheet** at the foot of your screen, and, by selecting this, the master page can be set up. Otherwise, it is likely to be accessible from the **New** dialog box.

Items from the following list are set up just once on the style sheet.

Margins
_____

Headers and Footers
_____

Page numbering
_____

Graphics or Logos
_____

Columns
_____

and any other recurring features of the document, including text style specifications which have been added to the style palette.

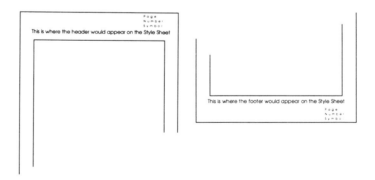

When preparing a Style Sheet any running Footers or Headers will appear on it just where you wish these to appear on the pages of the actual document. The symbol for the page numbers is also placed where these are to appear in the document.

A COVER

For this exercise, the left margin on the **Right Page** style sheet is 25 mm, while the right top and bottom margins are 20 mm. (Copy to **Facing Page** option is not needed in this exercise, as the cover will not be printed on the reverse but left blank.)

Typing directly onto the style sheet, type in the details below, using the specifications given.

HISTORY RECOVERED

Name	History
Size	30 pts
Font	Serif
Alignment	Left

Report by

Name	Report
Size	14 pts
Font	Sans Serif
Alignment	Left

Research Project

Same as **Report**, but Right

K Allen Department of Works

Name	Director
Size	12 pts
Font	Serif
Alignment	Right

The simple identifying logo is of 36 pts, serif, in a 1 pt frame, each character placed 8 mm apart. Matura MT Script Cap is the typeface used here, but any serif is acceptable.

Save as Covsty.??? in the appropriate directory. It would be useful to print out a copy of this information to have by your computer while you are completing the next two exercises.

*Style
sheet
cover*

HISTORY RECOVERED

Report by

Section

Research Project

K Allen Department of Works

▼ EXERCISE 31
TWO REPORT COVERS.

COVER FOR ORWELLS CASTLE REPORT

Recall the style sheet you saved as Covsty.??? in the last exercise. Ensure you are on page 1. You need to add the details which refer to the present cover.

120 mm down the left margin, type

ORWELLS CASTLE

Name	Building
Size	28 pts
Font	Serif, bold
Alignment	Left

Below that, and opposite 'Report by' (using **Report** specifications), type

Dervela McHugh

Below that, and opposite 'Section', type

10 Ballyfort

Save this document **As** Orcov.??? in the directory reserved for completed documents. **Print** one copy.

COVER FOR O'NEIL REPORT

Use the same style sheet (Covsty.???) for this exercise. Again working on page 1, the details for this particular cover are all that need to be added.

Using **Building** specifications, type

THE O'NEIL HOUSE

With **Report** specifications, type

Maurice O'Kane

With **Section** specifications, type

4 Farraway Area

Save As Onelcov.??? into the usual directory and **Print** one copy.

Using a style sheet

𝒟
𝒫
𝒲

HISTORY RECOVERED

ORWELLS CASTLE

Report by   Dervela McHugh

Section   10 Ballyfort

Research Project

K Allen Department of Works

HISTORY RECOVERED

THE O'NEIL HOUSE

Report by   Maurice O'Kane

Section   4 Farraway Area

Research Project

K Allen Department of Works

You can appreciate from these exercises how much work has been saved by having a style sheet which establishes all the details of the document and is, therefore, completed with the minimum input.

▼ Exercise 32
Image Control

In this exercise you will

1 **import images to be adjusted for lightness and contrast — image control**

2 **use large and mixed type sizes over the images**

Using design packages such as Adobe Illustrator, Corel Draw, and their respective Photo Shop extensions enables desktop publishers to extend their creativity. However, many desktop publishing programs do have the **image control** facility.

Image control also adds a variety of looks and finishes to an illustration, so that it can integrate more closely with the tone of the document being developed. As an example, there are times when a strong, high-contrast image is just right for one piece, while, as here, a softer, remote effect can be created.

The objective here is to control the image in relation to its darkness and contrast, so that text can be placed over it and read easily.

In this simple example, an image with a TIFF format was imported into the desktop publishing program, and, by selecting **Image Control**, the contrast was adjusted to a greyer effect. In this example, **Lightness** was 70 and **Contrast** 60. You should experiment with different values to obtain interesting results.

The font used throughout this document is Casper Openface, with the following specifications.

Main text is 24 pts

36 and 40 pts for the central title (where initial and last capitals are larger)

A 2 pt line above and below the smaller capitals

All text is centred.

Image control

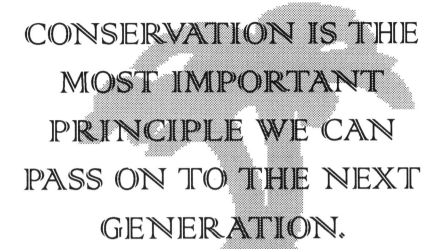

CONSERVATION IS THE
MOST IMPORTANT
PRINCIPLE WE CAN
PASS ON TO THE NEXT
GENERATION.

NATURE WATCH

WE NEED THE TREES,
THEIR LEAVES, THEIR
SHADE, THEIR COLOUR
AND FRUITS.
HUMANS AND ANIMALS
NEED THE TREES.

▼ EXERCISE 33
CUSTOMISING COLUMNS

Some documents cannot be set up with columns that are of unequal width unless you accept **Custom** at the Columns dialog box. You can then put in the widths you require, or accept the even options of two or more and manually move them on the electronic page. In this example, you will use two columns, the first 55 mm wide and the second 110 mm wide. Margins here are 20 mm all round. The gutter is 5 mm. Lock the column guides if you are able to do this. Import Examp.txt into the wide column.

Headline is serif, 28 pts, centre, graphic lines 1 pt.

The body text is serif, 12 pts, left aligned. Note, here, that the paragraph option is with indents, hyphenation is off and the space after each paragraph is 2 mm.

The sans serif text with bullets in the first column is 12 pts, with leading increased to 16 pts. The headings are emboldened. This text is to be input directly onto the electronic page from the example.

*Thumbnail
Exercise 33*

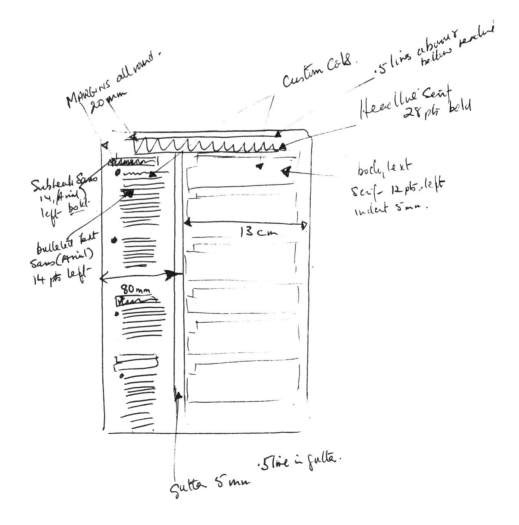

BEATING EXAMINATION PRESSURES

TWO POINTS OF VIEW

- This article outlines some of the problems facing students and pupils who do not prepare their schedule of study well enough.

- Advice is also given to help overcome the feeling of failure and helplessness.

HINTS ARE PROVIDED

- Several real-life situations are quoted to show that plenty can be done to ensure success and a sense of achievement.

YOU MAY BE THE ONE TO BENEFIT

- Be sure to follow the advice here for your mock and you will prove it can be done.

From January on students and Teachers make constant references to Examinations. Long before that examination bodies have set the papers as a result of meetings that had taken place early last year, and even before that someone somewhere decided to make changes or introduce a new examination or set out the papers differently.

Students are relaxed in September when they join a course after the long break and the thoughts of tests and study are far away. It may not be until the first essays are due to be handed up the reality strikes and genuine work has to be started. The academic year is very short with some years having an exceptionally short last term which is virtually packed with examinations. Many applicants for exams do not work early enough to give themselves the best chance to be in control of the situation. Instead they waste the early months and approach the exams with a poor grasp of practical and theoretical ability.

Not so the students of the Desktop Publishing Course. Many of them have produced work of an exceptionally high standard since November and from January on are perfecting their techniques so that as soon as they see the paper they know exactly what to do. Some even prepare sketches so that they can work from their own visuals once they have understood the requirements of the examination paper.

Examinations which need a lot of reading as preparation are often the ones students could do the most to improve in if they adopted a technique now recognised as a major factor in success in written exams - that is to spend short spells of time with frequent reference to the same texts as a learning aid. Frequency and recency it is called in the business.

Teachers are afraid that if the student body did learn like that some deep facts would be overlooked but this method does provide pegs for students to hang other facts on.

Many degrees and diplomas have been achieved by this method and it is felt that Second and Third level students would benefit by trying it too. There is expected to be a recommendation going out in the media very soon to catch those students who face the summer again this year with examinations on their minds. Notebooks and prompt lists are also a great help but nothing helps one learn as much as careful and regular reading, whatever the subject.

Writers of text books have made great efforts lately to provide excellent illustrations and clear paragraph headings for new topics to aid the learning process. Moves like this have helped so many students as well as careful note taking from these books.

▼ EXERCISE 34
COLOUR SEPARATIONS FOR SPOT COLOUR

1 BROSNAN PROMOTIONS

In this example, you will use one colour besides black. Although, in this book, only one colour and its tones are used, you may be able to use and print examples with two or more colours. Generally, spot colour is restricted to two colours per document, if it is a straightforward information piece. Decorative and artistic work would use more, but usually in these circumstances process colour is used. See page 177 for some information on printing in colour.

Black and purple are used to great advantage for this simple cover. At this stage in your course, you may not need detailed specifications, but below are the essential features.

Margins 20 mm all round

Purple frame 4 pts over this

Name   AvantGarde, 48 pts, left (60 pts initial capital)

Year   AvantGarde, 30 pts, left

The frame for the text is 75 mm x 90 mm. The top and bottom lines, only, have 4 pt lines in purple.

The text in the callout section is Ravel, 12 pts, left aligned, with hyphenation off. This is a relatively short piece and can be typed in the desktop publishing package.

Thumbnail Brosnan Promotions

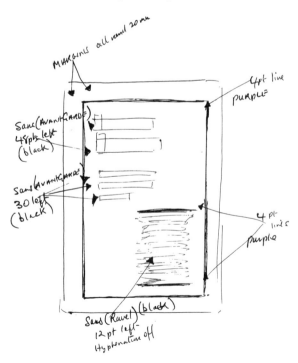

When you print this document on a colour printer, all the details will appear on one page if you select **Print**. If you are preparing it for a professional printer to make volume copies, plates will be needed of each colour and your in-house laser or inkjet will prepare masters for the printer to work from. Select **Separations** at the print dialog box. Printing this example, you will have two pages — one showing only the purple sections (the frame and lines) and the other showing the black text. On a black-only printer, you can request separations and get a sheet with just the black section and another with the purple (which, of course, will be in black).

BROSNAN PROMOTIONS

1996 PROGRAMME FOR DEVELOPING BANDS

Our exciting success in promoting music by up and coming bands has made us Europe's leaders in management. Bravo Boys and Palm Beaches, the smash hits of recent months, have proved how important it is to have experts behind every event and media contact. In this brochure you will find details of our trading policy and promotional system. We feel sure it's the right one for you.

Colour separations for spot colour – the complete page

BROSNAN PROMOTIONS

1996 PROGRAMME FOR DEVELOPING BANDS

Our exciting success in promoting music by up and coming bands has made us Europe's leaders in management. Bravo Boys and Palm Beaches, the smash hits of recent months, have proved how important it is to have experts behind every event and media contact. In this brochure you will find details of our trading policy and promotional system. We feel sure it's the right one for you.

Colour separations for spot colour – the black plate

*Colour separations
for spot colour –
the purple plate*

2 THE FUTURE OF COMPUTING

Again, in this example, two colours are used — black and purple, with text included in the spot colour.

This is an A4 document with 3 columns. Import and use as much of the HCI.txt as you need, cutting the remainder.

The purple headline — sans serif, Rounded M T, 36 pts and bold.

The purple text in column one — sans serif, Rounded M T, 18 pts, italic, with 40 pt leading.

Purple graphic lines are 4 pts.

Black text is serif, 20 pts in the headline, 12 pts justified in the main text.

Letter spaces can be used to move the headlines in a step sequence, or each line can be in its own text box for easy manoeuvring.

Select **Separations** before **Print** to get two pages, each with one colour if you are using a colour printer, and **Print** for a single sheet showing the whole document.

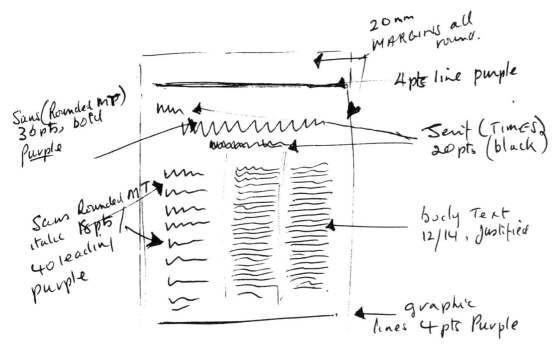

*Thumbnail
Future of computing*

*Colour
separations 2
the complete
page*

THE
FUTURE OF COMPUTING
for Technology Students

Marie Faulks,

Chief Executive

of Technoreach,

outlines the

likely future of

her company's

vision for com-

puting in the

coming years

Within the next eight to ten years I expect there to be many developments in the field of Human-computer interaction. I think one of the most important will be standardisation at the interface both in input by the user and in response by the computer.

I envisage much less keyboard use for strings of commands at input and an immediate move to the benefits of updated operating software which will offer a great improvement in the tone and range of its response. This update identifies the type of error made and has a less aggressive 'tone' in communicating with the user.

With regard to the keyboard itself I feel a move will have to be made before too long to get acceptance of a more suitable layout and possibly a design which includes a trackball or similar input device as a part of its surface. Steps like these would change the image of the computer from being 'shut off' and only available for specialist use, to its acceptance as a 'natural' part of business, functional and family life.

Even in homes it is housed in an office-like environment and when in a living or family room it is thought to be out of place. [I feel however, that the arrival of Minitel will shortly change this for us here as it has done for the French.]

I hope we can look forward to quick and easy access to computers with maybe varying levels of interaction once the 'novice' period has been passed. One major contribution to this objective would be an emphasis in hardware design for integration into ordinary family

Colour separations 2
— the black plate

THE

for Technology Students

Within the next eight to ten years I expect there to be many developments in the field of Human-computer interaction. I think one of the most important will be standardisation at the interface both in input by the user and in response by the computer.

I envisage much less keyboard use for strings of commands at input and an immediate move to the benefits of updated operating software which will offer a great improvement in the tone and range of its response. This update identifies the type of error made and has a less aggressive 'tone' in communicating with the user.

With regard to the keyboard itself I feel a move will have to be made before too long to get acceptance of a more suitable layout and possibly a design which includes a trackball or similar input device as a part of its surface. Steps like these would change the image of the computer from being 'shut off' and only available for specialist use, to its acceptance as a 'natural' part of business, functional and family life.

Even in homes it is housed in an office-like environment and when in a living or family room it is thought to be out of place. [I feel however, that the arrival of Minitel will shortly change this for us here as it has done for the French.]

I hope we can look forward to quick and easy access to computers with maybe varying levels of interaction once the 'novice' period has been passed. One major contribution to this objective would be an emphasis in hardware design for integration into ordinary family

Colour separations 2
— the purple plate

FUTURE OF COMPUTING

Marie Faulks,

Chief Executive

of Technoreach,

outlines the

likely future of

her company's

vision for com-

puting in the

coming years

▼ Exercise 35
Dropped Capitals (at Paragraph Starts)

A **drop cap**, as it is called, is placed at the beginning of lengthy text to add interest. It is not satisfactory to enlarge the first letter of the paragraph through the type size options, as this results in extra leading being applied to that line. Special features within the paragraph options usually allow you to select **First Character** and the number of lines deep that are to be dropped into. If this is not available to you, it is worth making each character that you wish to be a drop cap into a separate text block and placing that in a box you have created to keep the paragraph text away from that area. When you drag the larger character into place, you will have to kern the text to meet this as nearly as possible.

Fortunately, some packages have an extra facility which includes making drop caps, having marked the paragraph you wish to have enhanced. You need only specify the number of lines you wish to have affected.

For this exercise, set up 2 columns with 5 mm gutters. The text is available on your disk as Techno.txt. Flow the text into the two columns, removing any end-of-line spaces that may be in the text, and create paragraphs where they are in the exercise if they have been lost on importation.

The text specifications are as follows.

Headline text is 36 pts, left aligned.

Body text is 14 pts, serif, with 19 pt leading.

The space after paragraphs here is 2 mm.

The drop cap height is 48 pts, with kerning at 'Office' to bring the text closer to the larger character.

The graphic lines are 1 pt and the tint is 20%.

This example is part of a larger article that would have continued on a second page.

Dropped caps

THE FUTURE OF OUR WORK PLACE

Issue 21   Macrotext Ltd

Office Technology and how we as employees will fit into the new work pattern is a problem occupying many Human Resource consultants. Each component of this matrix has an individual part to play in communications as well as being a vital link in the chain of faster more efficient data exchange. We can see from the widespread use of Word Processing that computerisation has become the essential tool for administrative information gathering, output, and recording.

The integrated office system has been with us now for long enough for what used to be the slow interaction between one software package and another to take place on screen and almost simultaneously.

Data can be captured, stored, retrieved and reused in an entirely different package within seconds and by the same user. End users are increasingly imaginative with the use of the integrated package and develop personal routes and shortcuts to the desired objective.

The stand alone PC was eagerly accepted by many and abhorred by just as many employees. Just around the corner was the Network! This has called for a new attitude to work practices and what can be described as ownership of a project or part of it. Users may indeed be responsible for a particular part of, say, the design of a building, but interaction with others doing their part may be very limited, and involvement in the finished product when bringing it all together may not take place. Job satisfaction has to come from other areas than the finished design. The network has placed the responsibility for the technical integrity of the system in the hands of an expert who may or may not work in a hands-on role on the project.

Some users are much happier knowing that specialist help is on hand when problems to do with the system occur; however, some would like to deal with a network manager who understood the needs of users and the priorities they have in their work as well as the high standards they wish to reach.

Telecommunications advancements have impinged on all administrative staff. Not only have we seen an exceptional explosion in Telesales recently but there is an expectation that all employees will be conversant with Data bases provided by the country's competing Television and

▼ EXERCISE 36
A4 POSTER

The image is used to good advantage here, where the text is mostly within it and carefully placed to leave plenty of white space inside and outside. Several typefaces are used, though the serif and sans serif are reserved for particular uses. The alignment is mainly centred, but notice the left and right alignment at the foot of the poster.

A4 poster

THEATRE ENTERPRISES LIMITED

THE BEAUFORTE PLAYERS
PRESENT

**A STREETCAR NAMED
DESIRE**

BY
TENNESSEE WILLIAMS

Madelene Hughes
and
Jeremy Hanson
in the
leading roles

Elaine Maher and supporting
cast of fine actors from the
Beauforte Repertory Company

March 10 - 30
7 00 each weekday
3 00 pm and 8 00 pm Saturday
Tickets £10, £15 and £20
Group Booking Concessions

PHONE 7650031
BOX OFFICE
OPEN 11 00 - 8 00
Monday to Saturday
Credit Cards Welcome

▼ EXERCISE 37

MOCK-UP OF 3-COLUMN BROCHURE

This mock-up of a brochure becomes easier to assemble if a grid is established before anything is put on the page. The actual grid used is shown on page 74. Identify the elements which have to line up and place grid lines. Also, use Snap to Grid to ensure each text box or image is placed accurately. Remember that horizontal and vertical grid lines are needed here.

The frames and their contents at the top and bottom of each page, as well as the small images separating text, can be established once on the pasteboard and copied and pasted into position over the grid. The text here is separated by a wide standoff around each image to add an openness to what would otherwise be a dense and heavy-looking brochure. Import part of Newman.txt. This exercise is not developed to completion and leaves room for you to make changes and improvements to the details. The map can be imported or scanned from Appendix Seven or made up in a paint program or in a design program, saved as an image and then imported into the brochure.

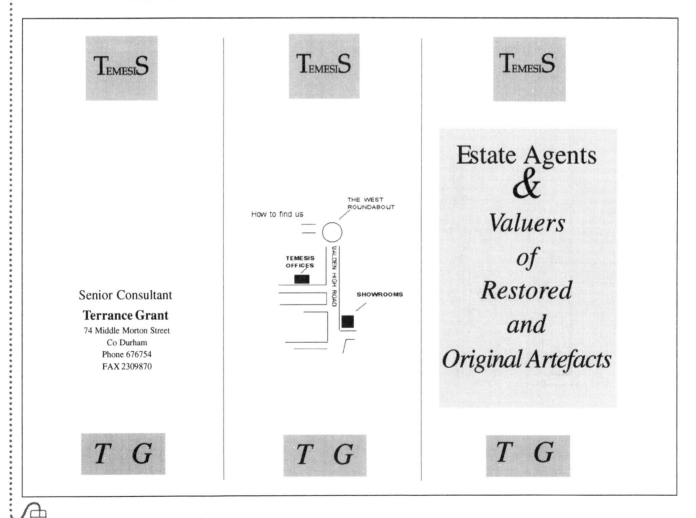

The preservation of Ireland's architectural heritage is widely accepted as a task of vital importance for the 1990s. Gallaher (Dublin) Limited has

modern University College Dublin. The property was later named Newman House in honour of the University's first rector John

series of lectures on the scope and nature of university education - the renowned discourses later published as The Idea of a University.

acknowledged the importance of this by giving its support to one of the country's leading conservation enterprises - the restoration of Newman House. The objectives of the project were threefold: to preserve for prosperity a unique and very beautiful building; to encourage excellence in contemporary Irish craftsmanship; and to bring to life again the architectural excellence.

Henry, Cardinal Newman. In 1755 Number 85 was purchased by Richard Chapel Whaley who also acquired the adjoining site and, in 1765, began building 86 St Stephen's Green. A rare wax portrait depicts Whaley with his young wife Anne Ward and their seven children. 'Buck' Whaley, the notorious rake and gambler, was the couple's second son. In

In one of his most famous passages Newman held forth a challenge and a prophecy for Ireland and for his university. James Joyce was a student of Philosophy and English at University College from 1899 to 1902. The old Physics Theatre of the University is located on the first floor of Number 85; it was in this room that Joyce gave his maiden speech to the Literary and Historical Society. Joyce later

Numbers 85 and 86 St Stephen's Green are two of the best and most original Georgian townhouses in Dublin. By good fortune these important buildings were united in common ownership in the mid-nineteenth century when acquired by the Catholic University of Ireland, the precursor of

the wax portrait he is depicted kneeling and holding a rattle to the right of the central group. In November of 1851 John Henry Newman was formally invited to become rector of new Catholic University of Ireland. In the following year Newman delivered a

used the Physics Theatre as a setting for an encounter in A Portrait of the Artist as a Young Man. In 1854 the newly established Catholic University of Ireland received its first students in Number 86 St Stephen's Green. The house has seen generations of students.

▼ EXERCISE 38

MULTI-PAGE DOCUMENT WITH TWO STYLE SHEETS

1   creating a style sheet for a news-sheet cover

2   creating a style sheet for the inside pages

3   using these style sheets

STYLE SHEET 1 — NEWS-SHEET COVER AND FIRST PAGE

The specifications for style sheet 1 are

Margins 20 mm all round

2 columns, 5 mm gutter

The type specifications (typefaces as near as possible to these will be adequate)

Name	Typeface	Size	Alignment
Head	Caslon Openface	28	force justify
Subs	sans serif, bold	14	left
Main	serif	12	left
Foot	sans serif, bold	12	centre
Call	Caslon Openface	14	centre

Page numbering is not required for page one of a newsletter, so it is not included in this style sheet.

Save As a style sheet called Comjnsty.???.

STYLE SHEET 2 — INSIDE PAGES

Prepare another style sheet for the inner pages of this multi-page document by modifying the previous one: remove the headline, Issue and Vol numbers, and create any new typefaces you may need for work of your own to follow the second article. If you intend to extend this article to several more pages, you should put page numbering in the bottom margin. (Select **starting at page 2.**) Automatic page numbering will put the correct numbers on all subsequent pages where you indicate on the style sheet.

Save As Cominsty.???.

USING STYLE SHEET 1

Recall Comjnsty.???. Import the text file HCI.txt onto page 1. Flow this into the two columns. There will be a considerable length of unused text, so retain this for use on the second style sheet (via the clipboard). Apply the text styles created on the style sheet and insert 4 at 'Issue' and 12 at 'Vol'. **Save As** Comjnl1.???.

USING STYLE SHEET 2

Using the inside pages style sheet Cominsty.???, flow the text from the clipboard into page 2, making sure that it is equally distributed between the two columns. Create a feature to define the second half of the page.

Create a callout with a standoff for this part of the page. Text for the callout is as follows.

TRENDS IN COMPUTING ASTOUND THE BEGINNER BUT ARE SECOND NATURE TO THE PROFESSIONAL

Apply the style **Call**.

Import Techno.txt, flowing this into the two columns and onto page three. You may have your own material which would work well under the two columns on page three. (If you have not, use any of the text supplied with this course.) Insert it here, under a heading, making sure it fits in with the style and tone of the rest of the document. **Save As** Compages.???. **Print** one copy and try printing page two on the back of page one, if your printer will accept paper that has already been through it.

*Multi-page with two style
sheets and continuing pages*

THE COMMUNICATIONS JOURNAL

ISSUE   VOL

THE COMMUNICATIONS INSTITUTE OF IRELAND

THE COMMUNICATIONS JOURNAL

ISSUE 4 VOL 12

Within the next eight to ten years I expect there to be many developments in the field of Human-computer interaction. I think one of the most important will be standardisation at the interface both in input by the user and in response by the computer.

I envisage much less keyboard use for strings of commands at input and an immediate move to the benefits of updated operating software which will offer a great improvement in the tone and range of its response. This update identifies the type of error made and has a less aggressive 'tone' in communicating with the user.

With regard to the keyboard itself I feel a move will have to be made before too long to get acceptance of a more suitable layout and possibly a design which includes a trackball or similar input device as a part of its surface. Steps like these would change the image of the computer from being 'shut off' and only available for specialist use, to its acceptance as a 'natural' part of business, functional and family life.

Even in homes it is housed in an office-like environment and when in a living or family room it is thought to be out of place. [I feel however, that the arrival of Minitel will shortly change this for us here as it has done for the French.]

I hope we can look forward to quick and easy access to computers with maybe varying levels of interaction once the 'novice' period has been passed. One major contribution to this objective would be an emphasis in hardware design for integration into ordinary family life: and we can point to telephone design as moving rapidly recently to fuller integration into decor of many types.

Another form of standardisation that is shortly to be expected is the high resolution screen with, of course, colour monitors. I feel the demand for Windows will account for the rapid move to high specification VDU's and I think Windows will provide the impetus for manufacturers to develop software for a much wider range of uses than we see at present of their life, together with children

being users much earlier than we have at present and using computers as a standard part of their homework and research for projects which is so much a part of a student's curriculum now.

I see Human-computer interaction providing a very wide range of interaction to services like Viewdata via educational resources like libraries simply because of the developments in telecommunications together with easier and attractive means of interaction with virtually error free routing to the user's goals. This would mean that the on-line help would have to be immediately available and executable just as easily if it was necessary at all. If computers could interpret the user's needs when an input error was made this whole area of side tracking for help could be avoided.

Eventually I see computers becoming an extension of our natural environment and being extraordinarily sensitive.

So far we use our eyes and fingers with keyboard and mouse for interaction but developments in the immediate future are likely to bring the full body into action with gesture, tracing of eye movements and changes in stance and head position being used as interactors. By comparison to the future we will seem to be very primitive. Virtual Reality is the environment for exploring the opportunities that total bodily involvement could create both as a working tool as at present in flight and space travel preparation and as a research tool to find out more about human behaviour. There is of course an expectation that Virtual Reality will provide a wide range of entertainment environments too.

Early in the history of the development of computers Hypertext and Powerbook were predicted by their developers to be of immense use. It seems that after all, this is just where Human-computer interaction is going now. Human-computer interaction will enable computers to

THE COMMUNICATIONS INSTITUTE OF IRELAND

become a very personalised tool enabling computers to recognise a wider and finer range of the user's behaviour - and hopefully be able to 'tune' its responses, as if trained, to the current session of interaction by reference to earlier sessions. I feel the linear use of computers which we have today will change to a tangential and cross referenced form of interaction which in itself can be mapped by the system to leave human beings to be more creative and less dependent on the spade work of life and leisure. [I wonder how the present Expert Systems with their inference engines will be seen in the light of developments in the fields I have just mentioned.]

At present the computer system and software developers dictate what is available to us - perhaps developments will enable a personal or family computer resource to interact with other systems just when the individual is ready to do so - in other words keep pace with individual developments

> **TRENDS IN COMPUTING ASTOUND THE BEGINNER BUT ARE SECOND NATURE TO THE PROFESSIONAL**

of personality and intellect and interest, opening up wider vistas as travel and television has for us up to now.

No survey of future developments in Human-computer interaction should end without a consideration of the range of interaction needed by the disabled. Already the breath, eyeblinks and chin movements are interfaced in education and on life-support levels. The inferencing interface mentioned above may be able to interpret unsteady users' movements, or a particular movement of trunk or limbs to good effect to influence their living and educational environment.

I would hope that speech and language learning for reading and communication skills for deaf and speech impaired users would be available so that the present laborious character, word and phrase building may be overtaken by software that creates clauses and sentences of a non-standard type for true conversation.

NEW WORKING SITUATIONS

Anyone entering an administrative environment should be fully conversant with what is called Office Technology. Each component of this matrix has an individual part to play in communications as well as being a vital link in the chain of faster more efficient data exchange.

We can see from the widespread use of Word Processing that computerisation has become the essential tool for administrative information gathering, output, and recording. The integrated office system has been with us now for long enough for what used to be the slow interaction between one software package and another to take place on screen and almost simultaneously. Data can be captured, stored, retrieved and reused in an entirely different package within seconds and by the same user.

End users are increasing imaginative with the use of the integrated package and develop personal

routes and shortcuts to the desired objective. The stand alone PC was eagerly accepted by many and abhorred by just as many employees. Just around the corner was the Network! This has called for a new attitude to work practices and what can be described as ownership of a project or part of it. Users may indeed be responsible for a particular part of, say, the design of a building, but interaction with others doing their part may be very limited, and involvement in the finished product when bringing it all together may not take place. Job satisfaction comes from other areas than the finished design.

The network has placed the responsibility for the technical integrity of the system in the hands of an expert who may or may not work in a hands-on role on the project. Some users are much happier knowing that specialist help is on hand when problems to do with the system occur; however, some would like to deal with a network manager who understood the needs of users and the priorities they have in their work load.

Telecommunications advancements have impinged on all administrative staff. Not only have we seen an exceptional explosion in Telesales recently but there is an expectation that all employees will be conversant with Data bases provided by the country's Television and Telecommunications service. So many companies rely on up to the minute information on currencies, credit ratings, sales figures, trends in markets, movement of goods and money that employees are expected to be able to retrieve this data from whatever source the company is linked to.

Some businesses stand or fall solely on the strengths of their computerised systems and their network capabilites, the travel industry for instance.

In this case we cannot imagine a successful venture unless mobile phones, fax machines, photocopiers, modems and computers work in tandem to provide the proprietor and their clients with communications facilities of the highest order.

Networks and telecommunications have brought widely spread organisations together in a way that ignores time and space differences. Local networks linked to others and linked via bridges to wider networks means that data captured in one location can be available in another part of the world and acted upon within minutes.

The social implications of these recent changes are wide indeed. As users and employees we can be forgiven at times if we are wary of interaction with people we are not face to face with. We may not be interacting with another person on the phone when voice recognition becomes more widely available. We may be booking our tickets for theatres and trains with pre-recorded voices which can interpret our requests and send out our order immediately. We may work more closely with people on other networks than with the people in the same building. This raises questions about the value we place on human interaction and increased preciousness of face to face communication and personal relationships.

Schools and parents should be aware of how different the world young people will be working in is from the one they went into and what limited chances there are in some employment for people to be themselves.

Your own work can go here and on the next page

Style Sheet

Page 1

Page 2

Page 3

*At print, choose **Thumbnails** to produce very small-scale pages, to check the overall appearance of a document*

▼ EXERCISE 39

A5 BROCHURE 1

This brochure is developed from an A4 landscape style sheet with the following specifications (though standard typefaces will also give pleasing results).

Margins 15 mm

2 columns with 5 mm gutters

Type specifications are

College	Bodoni, 30 pts
Course	France (kern 'Securities' to bring the 'i's closer), all centred
Course length	Bodoni, 16 pts

The inside text is Bodoni 16 pts, except the two lines at the foot of the page which are 12 pts and centred. Use tab stops where necessary to align the columns. The preset tabs will satisfy this requirement.

The tinted central stripe is a 40 mm wide rectangle the full length of the page, line to none and 20% tint (could be in colour).

The three text areas have rectangles round them, filled with paper, line to none and sent to back of text when in place. A triple 3 pt line is placed following the margins.

The reverse side is prepared on page 2 of the same file with the following specifications.

The margins on both pages are 20 mm for the outside and 30 mm for the inside. Each 'page' has two rectangles 20 mm wide the full length of the page, filled with 20% black, with 60 mm between them. The lines are removed from these rectangles, and from the paper-filled rectangles containing the course contents. In this example, both contents boxes are 80 mm x 100 mm. This is a variable dimension and can be altered from the master sheet as necessary for subsequent brochures, if the look of the finished product is improved by the change. (The second brochure in this series needs some small changes like this.)

All these details should be set up on a master or style sheet, as the next exercise will use almost identical repeating features for a brochure for a different course. **Save As** Morstyle.??? to denote a style sheet.

Recall this style sheet to input the text. This is probably best done on the desktop publishing page, as it is very scattered, short and variable. **Save** this two-page file **As** Mortec.???.

*Thumbnail
Exercise 39*

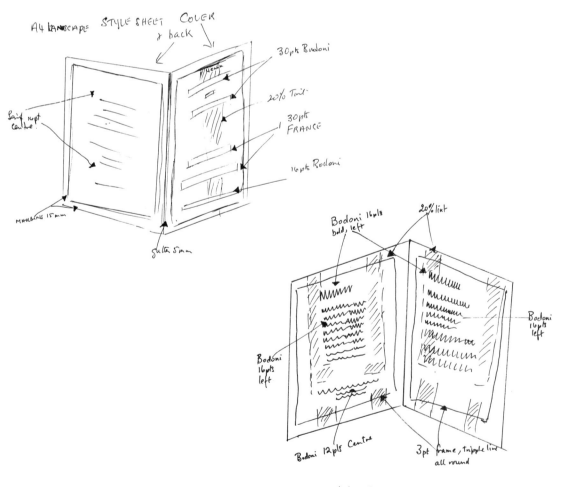

INSIDE

FOR DETAILS CONTACT
The Principal
Monica Hayes B.Sc. N H P Tech Ed.

Morehaven College of Technology
Stour Bridge
BARNSWICK
Tel 034 804081

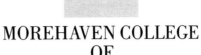

MOREHAVEN COLLEGE
OF
TECHNOLOGY

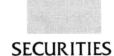

SECURITIES
MANAGEMENT

A ONE YEAR COURSE STARTING IN SEPTEMBER

*Inside
pages*

Course Contents

Accountancy Level II
Banking Level I
Mathematics Level 1
Communications Level I
French or German Level II
International Trading
 Practice Level I

Full Syllabus available from the Principal
or Course Director
Maurice J Flood

Application Procedure

Write, with a Self-Addressed
Envelope, for an application
form to the Secretary at the
address overleaf.

You should be available for
interview from April 1st and
have a detailed CV prepared
for the selection committee.

▼ EXERCISE 40
A5 BROCHURE 2

Recall the style sheet Morstyle.??? and insert the text provided in the example. Some changes will need to be made to the style sheet, such as enlarging the white areas. Save as Morart.???.

You can develop this exercise by drawing up details of another course that this college is likely to run, changing the names as well as the course contents.

Real-life assignments like these would require the desktop publisher to keep precise records and backups on disk for future use (which may be only once a year). It is useful, too, to include on the document a file name or date reference, as this type of publication could be used for dozens of similar courses or events in the same year (and, of course, it is the most recent file that should be updated).

MOREHAVEN COLLEGE
OF THE
PERFORMING ARTS

FOR DETAILS CONTACT
The Principal
P J Herron BA

FOLK ART
of the
20th CENTURY

Morehaven College of the Performing Arts
Stour Bridge
BARNSWICK
Tel 034 807752

A 20 WEEK COURSE STARTING IN SEPTEMBER

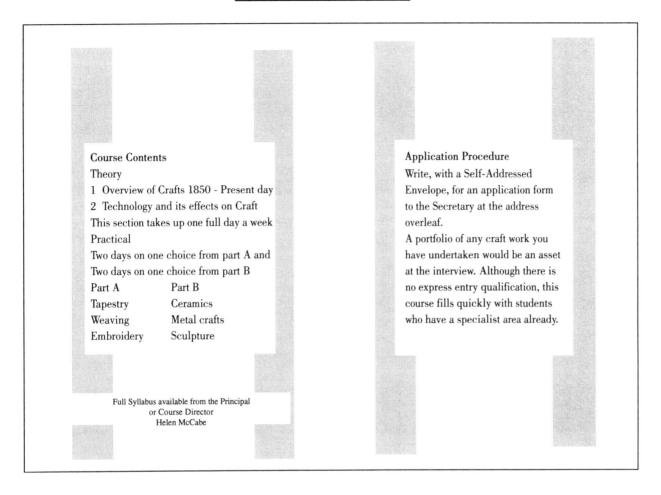

Course Contents
Theory
1 Overview of Crafts 1850 - Present day
2 Technology and its effects on Craft
This section takes up one full day a week
Practical
Two days on one choice from part A and
Two days on one choice from part B

Part A	Part B
Tapestry	Ceramics
Weaving	Metal crafts
Embroidery	Sculpture

Full Syllabus available from the Principal
or Course Director
Helen McCabe

Application Procedure
Write, with a Self-Addressed
Envelope, for an application form
to the Secretary at the address
overleaf.
A portfolio of any craft work you
have undertaken would be an asset
at the interview. Although there is
no express entry qualification, this
course fills quickly with students
who have a specialist area already.

▼ EXERCISE 41

2-COLUMN NEWS-SHEET, WITH DROP CAP AND CALLOUT

This single-page document could appear daunting to read if it were not made open and attractive to readers. Wider space between paragraphs is gained by setting a 2 mm 'space after' in the paragraph dialog box, and a callout is placed centrally, straddling the two columns.

TEXT SPECIFICATIONS

Headline	sans serif, 40 pts, bold, left aligned
Smaller details on right	sans serif, 14 pts, centred
Main text	serif, 12 pts with 14 pt leading, justified, with hyphenation off
Callout	sans serif, 14 pts, bold, centred, with 26 pt leading

GRAPHIC FEATURES

Headline fills	20% left and 10% right
Lines above and below callout	3 pts

The callout is created in a box, with line of none (in this case the dimensions are 70 mm wide and 60 mm deep). Triple lines are added to the top and bottom of this box.

Import Techno.txt (without concern for copy fitting here), using justified text.

This example lends itself to an enhancement of drop capitals. It is quite sufficient to have just two lines taken up with these — any deeper and they become too distracting.

*Thumbnail
Exercise 41*

FAXES & PHONES

MARGIN 20mm all round

fill 20%

San serif 40 pt bold left

fill 10%

Sans serif 14 pt, Centred

Two line Drop Cap

body text Serif 12pt/14 justified no hyphenation

3 pt line

Call out Sans 14 pt bold /26 leading, Centred

3pt double line

gutter 5mm

Callout with drop cap

FAXES AND PHONES

January 1996
The Voice of the Future
Supplement 19

Anyone entering an administrative environment should be fully conversant with what is called Office Technology. Each component of this matrix has an individual part to play in communications as well as being a vital link in the chain of faster more efficient data exchange.

We can see from the widespread use of Word Processing that computerisation has become the essential tool for administrative information gathering, output, and recording. The integrated office system has been with us now for long enough for what used to be the slow interaction between one software package and another to take place on screen and almost simultaneously. Data can be captured, stored, retrieved and reused in an entirely different package within seconds and by the same user. End users are increasingly imaginative with the use of the integrated package and develop personal routes and shortcuts to the desired objective.

The stand alone PC was eagerly accepted by many and abhorred by just as many employees. Just around the corner was the Network! This has called for a new attitude to work practices and what can be described as ownership of a project or part of it.

Users may indeed be responsible for a particular part of, say, the design of a building, but interaction with others doing their part may be very limited, and involvement in the finished product when bringing it all together may not take place. Job satisfaction comes from other areas than the finished design.

The network has placed the responsibility for the technical integrity of the system in the hands of an expert who may or may not work in a hands-on role on the project. Some users are much happier knowing that specialist help is on hand when problems to do with the system occur; however, some would like to deal with a network manager who understands the needs of users and the priorities they have in their work as well as the high standards they wish to reach.

Telecommunications advancements have impinged on all administrative staff. Not only have we seen an exceptional explosion in Telesales recently but there is an expectation that all employees will be conversant with Databases provided by the country's Television and Telecommunications service. So many companies rely on up to the minute information on currencies, credit ratings, sales figures, trends in markets, movement of goods and money that employees are expected to be able to retrieve this data from whatever source the company is linked to. Some businesses stand or fall just on the strengths of their computerised systems and their network capabilites, the travel industry for instance.

> Our future will be different - so much technology and they say so much time left over for leisure and pleasure. FAXES and PHONES to blame!

In this case we cannot imagine a successful venture unless mobile phones, fax machines, photocopiers, modems and computers work in tandem to provide the proprietor and their clients with communications facilities of the highest order.

Networks and telecommunications have brought widely spread organisations together in a way that ignores time and space differences. Local networks

· PART FOUR ·

CLIENT ORIGINATED ASSIGNMENTS AND LEVEL II EXAMINATION WORK

▼ EXERCISE 42

MOCK-UP OF A5 BOOKLET

This typical Level II assignment requires the application of standard text specifications to several text blocks, as well as the preparation of a style sheet.

The example you will work on is one booklet of a series being prepared to aid tourists. This particular one is about architectural renovations. You are to create an eight-page booklet from two A4 sheets which are folded in the middle. You cannot use automatic page numbering in the two-up requirement but you can put the number in from the keyboard on each page. The pages after the first (a right-hand page) will have no text on them, but all the items from the style sheet will be printed — header, footer and graphic lines, together with the page number that you put in. There is also to be a main heading, side heading, body text and a footnote — which you see is not the same as a footer!

Prepare the style sheet as an A4 landscape with two columns, each representing one page of the booklet. The gutter should be 25 mm and that is the inside margin on both pages and the fold. Set a margin of 15 mm all round for the other three sides.

Draw a graphic line across the top and bottom margin of 1 pt. Above this, type in the header

Guide To Centre City Locations September 1995

and place the footer

Modern History Series 4 Issue 2

below the bottom line. Repeat these details on both pages.

Set up the following specifications for the text which will appear on the first page only.

Header	serif, 12 pts, bold, left
Footer	sans serif, 10 pts, centre
Headline	serif, 18 pts, bold, centre
Paragraph heading	sans serif, 14 pts, left
Body text	serif, 12 pts, justified, hyphenation off and 2 mm between paragraphs
Footnote	serif, 10 pts, centre

The purpose of the mock-up is to give the client and production team a clearer idea of the finished look of the whole booklet (and therefore the series) and assess the time and cost involved in the project. At this stage, only the first page needs to be set.

Move to page one of the document and insert two more pages. This, in total, will give you eight pages of A5, printed on both sides.

Type in the main heading

A MAJOR NEW MOVE ON HISTORY

and the side headings

A Famous House Brought Back to Splendour

Spectacular Plaster Work

A Special Room

applying the styles created earlier.

In the assignment for which this example is to be worked, the requirement is that you prepare the text in a word processor yourself, spell check, save, and import it into the document. If you have not done so, you could use the text in this example of the mock-up, which requires you to correct, spell check and save, or you can import the text Architec.txt, cutting the portion you do not need. (This text is prepared specifically for the assignment and will therefore make sense.) You should make the text into paragraphs, so that they are ready to have the side headings applied to them. Put the two other headings before the next two paragraphs. Apply the styles to all the text sections. **Save As** Mockup???. **Print** one copy of the eight pages, which really requires you to re-insert the first page into the printer to get the second and seventh pages on the back of pages one and eight, and the back of pages three and six should show pages four and five. If your printer will not accept this routine, **Print** all the pages in one go and place them in the booklet in the correct order.

This assignment also requires you to provide a cover. It is worth preparing one in your desktop publishing package to complement the work you have put into this task. Create a new file for this — A4 landscape again, with two columns. You are only required to put the title and your name on the front. You can see from the sample how simple it can be. On the other hand, it can be made much more attractive by using the techniques and enhancements you have learned in this course. **Save As** Mockcov.???. **Print** one copy. The cover is to be folded and wrapped round the booklet.

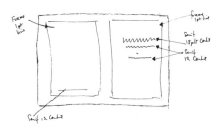

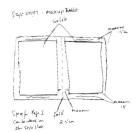

Thumbnail Exercise 42

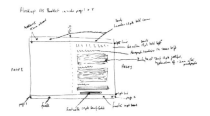

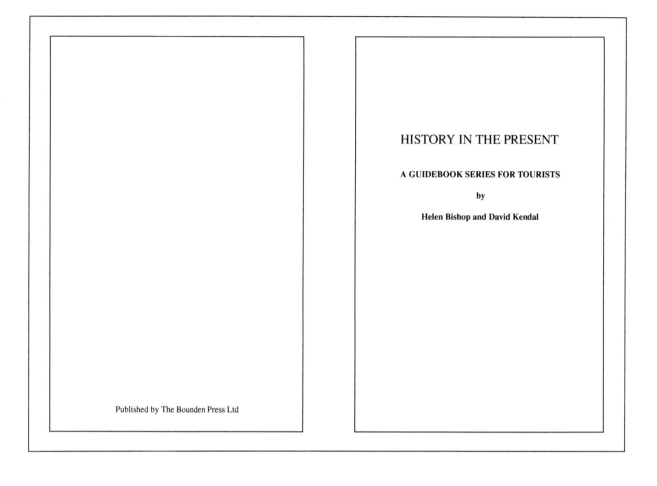

HISTORY IN THE PRESENT

A GUIDEBOOK SERIES FOR TOURISTS

by

Helen Bishop and David Kendal

Published by The Bounden Press Ltd

A MAJOR NEW MOVE ON HISTORY

A Famous House Brought Back to Splendour

The restoration of the Saloon and stairhall of Number 85 was commenced in January 1992. Throughout 1992 and 1993 thorough research and conservation was carried out in order to return these interiors to their early eighteenth-century appearance. The plasterwork was carefully cleaned and the original colour scheme has now been reinstated.

Two of the many features of this superb Georgian house are the Saloon and grand stairhall.

Spectactular Plaster Work

Particularly noteworthy is the lavishly decorated plasterwork of the Saloon, initially created by the Swiss stuccodore Paolo and Filippo Lafranchini. The project has rekindled the spirit of Georgian craftsmanship and is recognised as a unique achievement of architectural and historical importance. Gallaher (Dublin) Limited is proud to have been involved as patron in preserving this vital part of our national heritage.

Number 85 St Stephen's Green is attributed to Richard Castle,* Ireland's leading Palladian designer of the mid-eighteenth century. The grandest and most consciously architectural interior in Newman House is the Saloon on the first floor of Number 85 St Stephen's Green. Especially noteworthy is the room's coved ceiling which is decorated with a figurative plasterwork scheme.

A Special Room

The Apollo room is a diminutive interior with stucco decoration by the Lafranchini brothers. The decorative scheme depicts Apollo, god of arts, surrounded by the nine muses of the arts.

* See "History of A Famous Residence" p 90, 1930 edition

1

Guide To Centre City Locations   September 1995   Guide To Centre City Locations   September 1995

A MAJOR NEW MOVE ON HISTORY

A Famous House Brought Back to Splendor

The restoration of the Saloon and stairhall of Number 85 was commenced in January 1992. Throughout 1992 and 1993 thorough research and conservation was carried out in order to return these interiors to their early eighteenth-century appearance. The plasterwork was carefully cleaned and the original colour scheme has now been reinstated.

Two of the many features of this superb Georgian house are the Saloon and grand stairhall.

Spectacflar Plaster Work

Particularly noteworthy is the lavishly decorated plasterwork of the Saloon, initially created by the Swiss stuccodore Paolo and Filippo Lafranchini. The project has rekindled the spirit of Georgian craftsmanship and is recognised as a unique achievement of architectural and historical importance. Gallaher (Dublin) Limited is proud to have been involved as patron in preserving this vital part of our national heritage.

Number 85 St Stephen's Green is attributed to Richard Castle,* Ireland's leading Palladian designer of the mid-eighteenth century. The grandest and most conspicuously architectural interior is Newman House is the Saloon on the first floor of Number 85 St Stephen's Green. Especially noteworthy is the room's coved ceiling which is decorated with a figurative plasterwork scheme.

A Special Room

The Apollo room is a diminutive interior with stucco decoration by the Lafranchini brothers. The decorative scheme depicts Apollo, god of arts, surrounded by the nine muses of the

* See "History of A Famous Residence" p 90, 1930 edition

2

Guide To Centre City Locations   September 1995   Guide To Centre City Locations   September 1995

3

Guide To Centre City Locations   September 1995   Guide To Centre City Locations   September 1995

4

Guide To Centre City Locations   September 1995   Guide To Centre City Locations   September 1995

5

Guide To Centre City Locations   September 1995   Guide To Centre City Locations   September 1995

▼ EXERCISE 43

NEWS-SHEET WITH 3 COLUMNS AND CALLOUT

In this typical news-sheet layout, the interest depends on the callout and the addition of graphic lines. These are best kept to .5 for the top and 4 pts for the lower and callout double lines.

You can develop this exercise to run onto another page, as there is sufficient text for that. You should retain the three-column layout for the completion of this article and, if there is any space below it (remember to keep the columns of equal length), input another text using different features of presentation, like typeface and column width.

3-column news-sheet with callout

RESTORATION NEWS

Quarterly Magazine of the Architectural World   *Centenary Edition*

The preservation of Ireland's architectural heritage is widely accepted as a task of vital importance for the 1990's. Gallaher (Dublin) Limited has acknowledged the importance of this by giving its support to one of the country's leading conservation enterprises - the restoration of Newman House.

The objectives of the project were threefold: to preserve for prosperity a unique and very beautiful building; to encourage excellence in contemporary Irish craftsmanship; and to bring to life again its architectural excellence.

Numbers 85 and 86 St Stephen's Green are two of the best and most original Georgian townhouses in Dublin. By good fortune these important buildings were united in common ownership in the mid-nineteenth century when acquired by the Catholic University of Ireland, the

precursor of modern University College Dublin. The property was later named Newman House in honour of the University's first rector John Henry, Cardinal Newman. In 1755 Number 85 was purchased by Richard Chapel Whaley who also acquired the adjoining site and, in 1765, began building 86 St Stephen's Green.

A rare wax portrait depicts Whaley with his young wife Anne Ward and their seven children. 'Buck' Whaley, the notorious rake and gambler, was the couple's second son. In the wax portrait he is depicted kneeling and holding a rattle to the right of the central group.

In November of 1851 John Henry Newman was formally invited to become rector of the new Catholic University of Ireland. In the following year Newman delivered a series of lectures on the scope and nature of university education - the renowned discourses later published as The Idea of a

First Students at Number 86 St Stephen's Green in 1854

University. In one of his most famous passages Newman held forth a challenge and a prophecy for Ireland and for his university.

James Joyce was a student of Philosophy and English at University College from 1899 to 1902. The old Physics Theatre of the University is located on the first floor of Number 85; it was in this room that Joyce gave his maiden speech to the Literary and Historical Society.

Joyce later used the Physics Theatre as a setting for an encounter in A Portrait of the Artist as a Young Man. In 1854 the newly established Catholic University of Ireland received its first students in Number 86 St Stephen's Green.

Since this time the house has seen successive generations of students. The worn threshold of Number 86 is an evocative image for many graduates with fond memories of the building.

In 1884 the English poet and Jesuit priest Gerard Manley Hopkins, was appointed Professor of Classics at University College. While in Dublin Hopkins wrote the se-

▼ EXERCISE 44

A3 (OR A4) POSTER FOR A HOTEL ADVERTISEMENT

This design is suited to A3 and can be tiled on printout for you to have an idea of the finished product. Of course, setting it up as an A4 is just as valuable an exercise.

The interesting feature of this example is that the text across the top is 'text as a graphic'. It was created in Word 6 from the Wordart option and pasted via the clipboard into the advertisement. Any striking image will suit, if this cannot be scanned and cleaned up for importation from the sample here. The dynamic effect is achieved because the image and the text extend beyond the tinted circle. In this instance, the tint of the circle is a colour tint, which gives a greater range of density than the Fill option. The original butterfly was coloured and a tone from the wings chosen to fill the circle. Note also that, apart from the logo text, there are only three fonts used here, and all of these appear in the leaflet in the next exercise.

A3/A4 poster

▼ EXERCISE 45

A5 LEAFLET FOR ACTIVITY HOLIDAYS

This A5 leaflet was designed to be left in tourist offices, libraries and hotel reception areas. It had to be informative and attractive. Only one sheet of the leaflet is shown in the exercise, the cover and back.

A two-column grid was set up, with the frames created for one side and copied to the other. Tints as fills were 20% of a colour edited from the colour palette. The image has been mirrored for the back cover. The right-hand side of this document repeats the logo, typeface and tint from the previous exercise, confirming how important the initial decision about these features is. They are likely to be associated with all documents used by that hotel and have to be suitable for a variety of situations.

A5 brochure

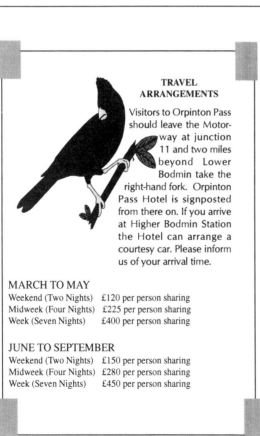

TRAVEL ARRANGEMENTS

Visitors to Orpinton Pass should leave the Motorway at junction 11 and two miles beyond Lower Bodmin take the right-hand fork. Orpinton Pass Hotel is signposted from there on. If you arrive at Higher Bodmin Station the Hotel can arrange a courtesy car. Please inform us of your arrival time.

MARCH TO MAY

Weekend (Two Nights)   £120 per person sharing
Midweek (Four Nights) £225 per person sharing
Week (Seven Nights)   £400 per person sharing

JUNE TO SEPTEMBER

Weekend (Two Nights)   £150 per person sharing
Midweek (Four Nights) £280 per person sharing
Week (Seven Nights)   £450 per person sharing

ORPINTON PASS HOTEL

Activity
Holidays
Spring & Summer

Phone 100 3737259
Martin or Denise will answer any queries you may have

▼ EXERCISE 46
ACETATES FOR OVERHEAD PROJECTORS

Many presentations require acetates for overhead projection. Today nearly all in-house printers, laser and ink-jet, will print onto *quality* acetate sheets. A feature of many presentations is that, although they are verbal, they are backed up by visuals to aid memory and add interest. Very effective visuals can be made in-house by careful selection of simple text, white space and colour (if available) or tints and fills. The presentations are often repeated to different groups, so it is worth spending time getting them right. Each sheet should be numbered to help the presenter keep track of the series. The company logo is usually on every sheet and there are often recurring features on each sheet. Thus, acetates lend themselves to setting up a style sheet showing margins, type styles, logos and other recurring details.

In the examples here, the central textual details change but much of the rest is constant. Set up a style sheet with the recurring features and **Save As** OHPmast.???. Then use it to create Number 1. **Save As** OHP1.???. Recall a copy of the style sheet and use that to create the second in the series. You could continue the series making the topic of the third COST EFFECTIVE MEASURES 1995, using either text or chart forms. Remember that you can import charts and sections of spreadsheets into your desktop publishing program as well. Use your skills to make this chart more dimensional and interesting than the ones shown here. These exercises link in with the supplementary exercise on Company Stationery (exercise 27).

Thumbnail
Exercise 46

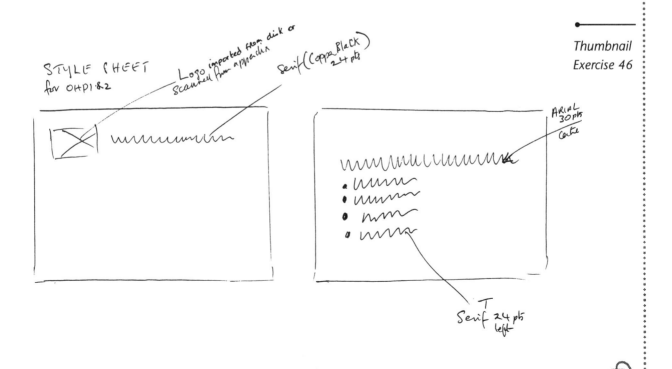

*Thumbnail
Exercise 46*

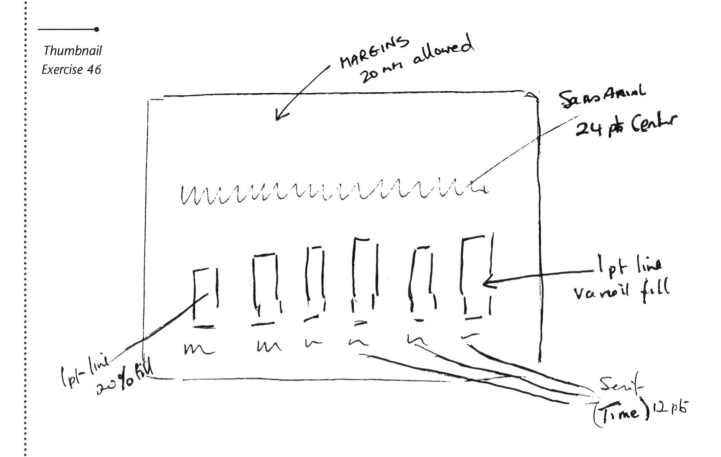

MARGINS 20 mm allowed

Sans Arial 24 pt Centr

1 pt line vairoil fill

1 pt line 20% fill

Serif (Time) 12 pts

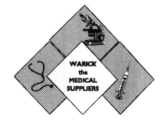

WARICK MEDICAL SUPPLIERS PLC

WARICK the MEDICAL SUPPLIERS

COMPANY DEVELOPMENT SINCE 1994

- **Exports increased by 15%**

- **Home sales increased by 21%**

- **Reduction in overheads 5%**

- **Relocation costs £20,000 below estimate**

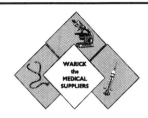

WARICK MEDICAL SUPPLIERS PLC

GROWTH IN MEDICAL SUPPLIES TO HOSPITALS 1995

 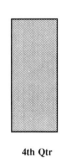 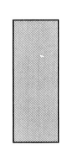    

| 3rd Qtr 1994 | 4th Qtr 1994 | 1sr Qtr 1995 | 2nd Qtr 1995 | 3rd Qtr 1995 | 4th Qtr 1995 | 1st Qtr 1996 PROJECTED |

▼ EXERCISE 47
GATEFOLD BROCHURE

This gatefold brochure is double sided. A page with three equal columns with narrow gutters and margins of 5 mm all round is set up.

PAGE ONE

This contains the front fold, the back panel, and the last page. Import House.txt. This text starts in column three of page one and continues on page two in column one, two and three, finishing in column 1 on page two! Very careful attention to placement and proofreading is essential to keep the correct order. This is an instance when having a hard copy of the text to refer to helps the production process. You will find this in Appendix Six.

(The text in this design has been edited slightly to provide for easier reading at the bullets.)

Three type styles are used

Title box	sans serif, 24 pts, centre
Front text	16 pts (Vogue used here), italic, leading 32 pts, justified
Main text	14 pts (Vogue), leading 28 pts, left aligned

Back panel specifications

Name	sans serif, 16 pts, left, bold
Address	sans serif, 12 pts, left, bold

The logo is simply the initials as text objects placed, as shown, in very close view and then copied and pasted to next page.

Sometimes the most suitable illustrations have to be hand-drawn and scanned in, as is the case here. However, any suitable image file would serve for class purposes if this drawing cannot be emulated and scanned, and, of course, do not reject the conventional cut and paste where special artwork is physically pasted into the document. It is available on the disk provided.

PAGE TWO

The careful placement of the text at the top of each column is intentionally not maintained at the foot of the columns, to give enough text in each while aiming at a self-contained section in each.

FURTHER EXERCISE

As a follow-up exercise, you should retain the same orientation, margins and gutters, as well as the same text, to develop an entirely new look to the brochure. Research images, maps and logos which would make the brochure more interesting by breaking up the text.

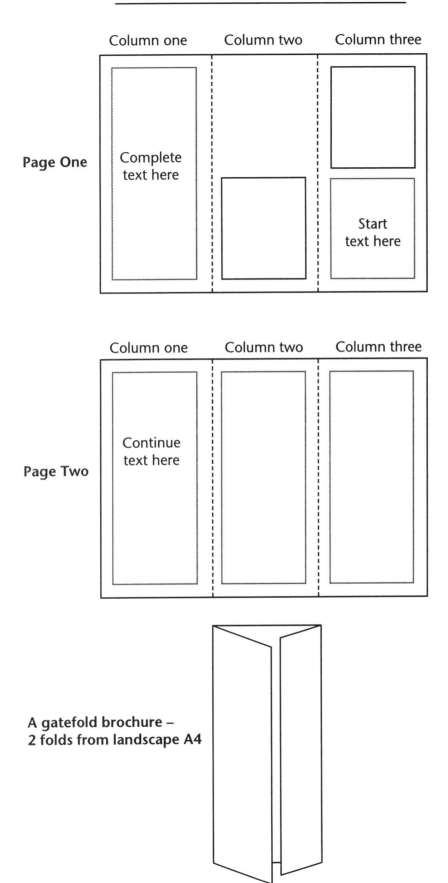

Diagram for fold and text flow

Gatefold brochure

Apartments like these rarely come on the market. These have all been developed from a widely accepted formula that has sold well for the last four years but given individuality by being personalized for this site. This means that wherever possible, the living room has been placed to give the best view or the best light as a priority and the other rooms designed to lead from this while bedrooms are accessed from another direction. There are landscape features to the apartments but in keeping with the open aspect of the site as a whole.

The properties in all three categories are Gas Fired Centrally Heated and open fireplaces are a standard in all living rooms. Interior decor has been designed by **Phillip Ketchly and Company** and your individual needs can be met in consultation with one of his representatives.

Call
MORRISON & PRENTICE
112 White Hart Lane
Bullmead Cheshire

M
P

Builders of Distinction
Phone 37 3755001
FAX   37 3709813

This development is being undertaken by the country's most experienced architect and builders working as a team from the initial stages of planning to the completion of the property.

The original site has been secured many years ago but left in the hands of the occupants until the demise of the leaseholder. During that time several overall plans had been devised and worked on in outline only.

Eventually, taking into account the developments in the surrounding areas, one of these early plans was chosen. Builder and Architect applied the most advanced tehniques to every aspect of this huge undertaking from enclosing the site from the ajoining properties to its promotion on completion.

There are three types of property on this undulating site, each development given unique views and approaches to the countryside and infra structure:-
Entering The Coopers Yard

● **The three-storey houses** can only be described as modern but adhering to the traditional qualities of family and community living. There are facilities for car parking, garaging, storage and field games without having all on view. Carefully designed areas of foliage and

grass give openness and freedom to those who wish to have access to the countryside.

● **Two-storey terraced houses** form an unusual feature of this area with just 52 units divided between the four sites. These are mainly two-bedroom houses with eight three-bedroom styles in the area near the apartment block.

● **The three-bedroom property** has the expected standards of finish to all kitchen bathroom and ensuite fitments being designed by **Hall and Harris** especially for this development.

▼ Exercise 48
A Book Jacket

The dimensions for this jacket are as follows.

Select Custom and **Wide**, with 320 mm across and 200 mm down. There will be three columns, but of custom width. Most packages will enable you to set any number of columns and then move them manually. You should adjust yours to be

Column 1   150 mm wide

Column 2   20 mm wide

Column 3   150 mm wide

Margins of 5 mm all round.

Columns 2 and 3 are filled with a 10% tint of purple.

The bar code space can be left empty or one can be scanned in, as here.

This very simple design should be constructed on a style sheet and then the saved master can be used for designs of interesting typography and image combination for book titles you make up yourself.

Type Specifications

Title   initial caps 60 pts, and 48 pts for remaining text, with the last word rotated 45 degrees.

Press comment on front 18 pts. In this example, the 'ITY' sequence of letters was kerned to give slightly wider space between them. You should research a suitable image which could be scanned and adapted in a paint program to fit neatly round the text or use the image on the disk provided.

The spine of the book has a smaller version (20 pts) of the title and a simple logo which you can copy (or develop one of your own).

The press comments, or blurbs, were prepared in a word processor and imported — 14 pts with some italics. Note the use of quotes in this text. Typographers' quotes* have been used to give a professional appearance. **Save As** Fratcov.???. **Print** with **Reduce to Fit** selected in the print dialog box if you want to see it on A4, and tile if you want it in the correct size but produced on overlapping sheets.

*Usually available from Preferences in File menu.

*Thumbnail
Exercise 48*

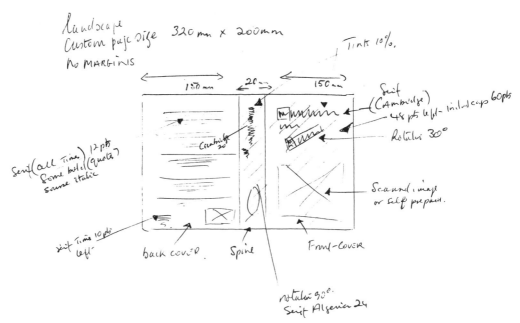

Bookjacket

Landscape
Custom page size 320mm x 200mm
No MARGINS

Tint 10%

150 mm   20 mm   150 mm

Serif (Cambridge)
48 pts left - initial caps 60pts

Rotate 30°

Cambridge
20

Serif (all Times) 12pts
from text (quotes)
source italic

Scanned image
or self prepared.

Serif Times 10pts
left

back cover.   Spine   Front-cover

rotate 90°.
Serif Algeria 24

*Landscape custom-
sized bookjacket*

Ms Hare has a long-standing reputation for producing tantilising novels. This is what the Press had to say about Ms Hare's latest work -

"An exotic setting for a novel of ruthless romance and crime"
The Daily Herald - G Monroe

"This novel has to be read - the city and its Mafia associations are cleverly interwoven with love and abandonment."
The Reader's Companion - Leslie Hart

"The far-reaching events of a holiday in Venice are explored in the exciting and sharp writing of Magenta Hare."
The Times Literary Correspondent - Gerald P Homer

"Writing like this is seldom poured into a tale of intrigue and passion - do read it at once."
Writing Today - Penny Wrathers

$12.95 USA
£6.25   UK and Ireland

ISBN 1-85471-600-X

9 781854 716002

FRATERNITY OF LOVE

MILLER & CROON

FRATERNITY OF LOVE

by

Magenta Hare

THIS SEASON'S BLOCK BUSTER

▼ EXERCISE 49
MUSEUM FACSIMILE

The page measurements for this document are 120 mm wide and 205 mm deep. The text has been adapted from Museum.txt, supplied with the book, although you can use it as it comes. The interest here is in the combination of typeface, size, leading and initial capitals. You may have a typeface with a gothic feel to it, or even an Irish typeface, which would be even more appropriate for the main text, while the initial letters would have to be in a very large point size to add the emphasis that is in this example.

*Thumbnail
Exercise 49
Custom
page size*

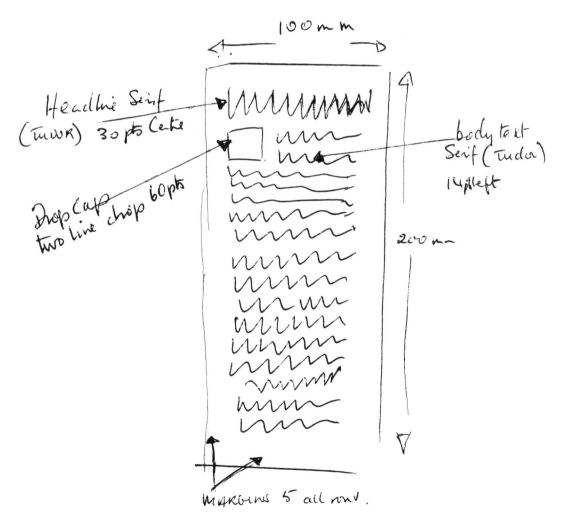

European Design

The early Christian period was very influential: designers looked at the church plate and jewellery which survived from that period. A large number of ancient architectural remains from across Europe were also studied. Most importantly they studied ancient manuscripts for information about French civilization and history. Another vital asset was that a common language was still intact. They found that the French people were inspired by songs and telling stories and the cultures of many European people were also drawn upon. "People who had been told for years that these were savages with a barbarous language and no evidence of civilization were persuaded that it was not so."

▼ EXERCISE 50
FRONT COVER FOR A4 MAGAZINE

The whole piece depends on elemental shapes with tints and fills in a variety of densities. There is a perspective in this example, with the dense fill of the Courts in the foreground. Simplicity is the key to the almost total serif text for this formal context.

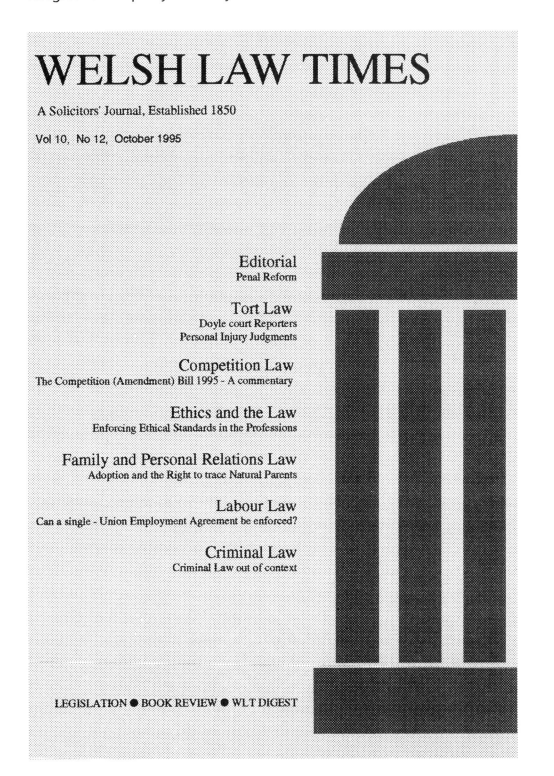

WELSH LAW TIMES

A Solicitors' Journal, Established 1850

Vol 10, No 12, October 1995

Editorial
Penal Reform

Tort Law
Doyle court Reporters
Personal Injury Judgments

Competition Law
The Competition (Amendment) Bill 1995 - A commentary

Ethics and the Law
Enforcing Ethical Standards in the Professions

Family and Personal Relations Law
Adoption and the Right to trace Natural Parents

Labour Law
Can a single - Union Employment Agreement be enforced?

Criminal Law
Criminal Law out of context

LEGISLATION ● BOOK REVIEW ● WLT DIGEST

▼ EXERCISE 51

BACK COVER FOR A4 MAGAZINE

Here is a purely informative piece, requiring careful assembly of paper-filled rectangles and shadows. Once one has been constructed, it can be copied and pasted. Notice that the top rectangle has a shadow placed to separate it from the others and therefore needs individual construction. The text across the top is imported in two parts from Word 6 as Wordart to form an undulating line. Note, too, the simple sans serif text in the white boxes which is organised to be readable rather than be consistent in position.

A4 magazine back cover using a wide range of tints

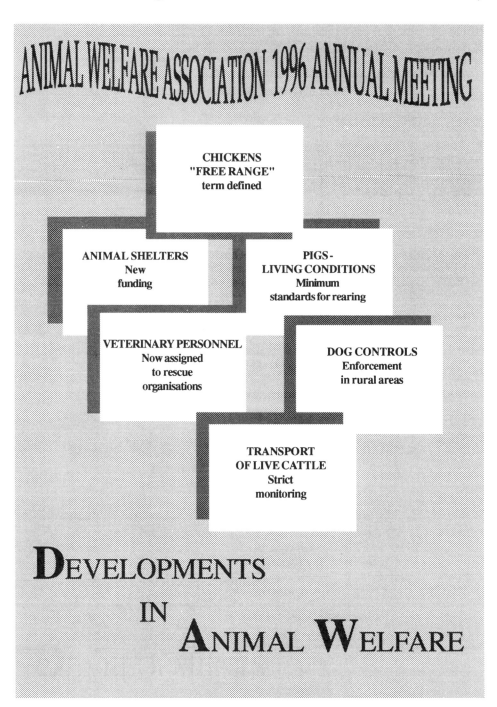

NOTICES AND POSTERS

The last four exercises of the book require detailed plans and lengthy sessions at the computer to create notices and posters. Remember to save often. Several of these assignments lend themselves to being output to either A4 or A3. Before you start, you must decide what size your document is intended to be, so that you choose the correct type sizes. Although you can scale at print time both up and down, it is very important to have some work in your portfolio that is designed for A3 and printed out tiled.

It is a requirement for an assignment of the City and Guilds Level II that an A3 poster be created. The brief is only specific in requiring students to have designs for the topics given and, included in these designs, bullets, raised or drop caps, among other features, as well as a scanned image and some text. The samples and exercises shown here will meet all these specifications over several documents.

▼ EXERCISE 52
A NOTICE

An eye-catching notice on A4

This is a complex exercise to accomplish solely within the desktop publishing package, and it may be easier to construct the 'cards' in a design package and import them for placement. Saving the design as an independent image enables you to use it in other situations and it is easily adaptable to new demands once the creation part is over. The text in this piece is purposely kept to a minimum, as the target audience needs to get this information without distraction.

EMPLOYMENT SEEKERS REMEMBER THESE VITAL POINTS:

KEEP YOUR CURRICULUM VITAE UP TO DATE

Make it specific for each application

COPY ALL THE LETTERS YOU SEND

and keep a record of telephone calls made with dates

Make sure you remember the names of those to whom you speak when you phone a company

BE ORGANISED!

▼ EXERCISE 53
ANOTHER NOTICE OR POSTER

Many examples in this book use low-density fills to add interest to a document. The background and frame image in this example was originated in a basic paint program, with the pencil tool drawing an irregular wide line (over a rectangle to serve as a guide). The low-density fill is any pale colour, which can be edited after you have seen the first draft, while the line is a medium colour, giving a less startling contrast than black. Obviously, this would print out well on a colour printer, but can also be output to a monochrome printer. The whole image of border and fill was saved as a TIFF file, so that further contrasting variations can be made within the desktop publishing package. This file serves as a master for any similar flyer or document which would benefit from this format. Keep in mind that this is now an image that can be sized and edited in future.

The typeface used here is Caslon Openface, although any serif would be a good substitute. This example demonstrates that dealing with text in separate blocks is often the quickest way to achieve flexibility and manoeuvrability if various layouts are to be tried, or when minor adjustments in placement are necessary.

▼ EXERCISE 54
GREETINGS CARD

Use the image created in the last assignment for this exercise.

Prepare a small greetings card which clients would have the florist send with the flowers they order. Small here means A6 (150 mm x 100 m), folded centrally, so you will need to reduce everything considerably. The inside can be left blank for the message, or decorated as you feel best.

*Imported graphic
background and
image in a simple
advertisement*

▼ EXERCISE 55

POSTER WITH GRAPHICS

The graphic features of this example are simply a rectangle 60 mm wide filled with a 30% fill, a circle 60 mm in diameter, 30% filled, placed behind the rectangle, and both with lines to none. These two shapes are alternated with a 60 mm rectangle, 20% filled, and a central 20 mm rectangle filled with paper. When one section is assembled, it is copied and pasted across the top of the page. This whole design can be done even more easily in a design-type package, where the parts can be grouped for copy and pasting and grouped again, and exported as a TIFF or PCX and then imported into the desktop publishing document, where it can be subjected to image control to give a variety of effects.

In this example, the font used is France, but any serif typeface would be suitable.

Sizes range from 80 pts for Bangor, 48 pts for most of the text and 30 for the last line. Each line is in its own text box for easy placement.

A3/A4 poster with graphics

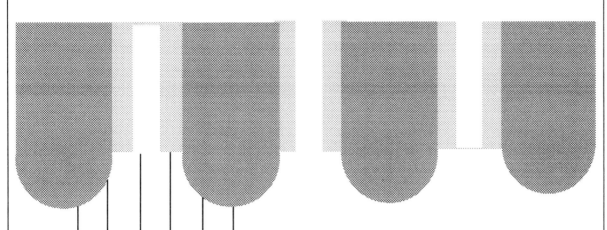

BANGOR

THE MODERN MARINA

EVERY FACILITY FOR ALL CRAFT

CHILDREN'S PLAY AREA

TEMPORARY BERTHS

PERMANENT BERTHS

FABULOUS PROMENADE

APPLY TO THE HARBOUR MASTER FOR FURTHER DETAILS

EIGHT ASSIGNMENTS FOR DEVELOPING YOUR SKILLS

These assignments are taken from real-life briefs that agencies are frequently asked to work on. There are no detailed specifications, but you are expected to observe the guidelines of good presentation that underlie this course.

You will probably have to do considerable research to achieve satisfying results, but keep your notes, as they can often be used for other projects. Design — first as sketches or roughs on paper — several possibilities for the following. Choose the most suitable and set up a page design for each in your desktop publishing package. You will usually have to set up Custom size at Page Setup, and at print time use scaling for over A4 items and crop marks for under A4 designs, to see more clearly what the finished product will look like.

1   A **form** for a Residents' Association that will be used to collect the quarterly subscription. (A5, one image.)

2   The **cover** for the sheets of a Wedding Service. (Here the typography and images are of greatest consideration.)

3   A museum specialising in archaeological finds requires, among other items for sale in its museum shop, a **bookmark** promoting its latest exhibition. (The size here is 75 mm x 280 mm.)

4   A chain of clothes retailers for the younger set (20 – 35 years) is updating its **logo**. This will appear on its carrier bags and stationery and form part of its facia board, as well as on all other company statements. The company trades as Style Monaco. You are free to design the logo in whatever style you wish. (Upper and lower case, or mixtures of these and type styles.) Remember that this logo will appear in a wide variety of sizes, places and materials, so the ordinary printing process is not the only consideration.

5   The Morehaven Arts Festival requires a design for **tickets** for all its events. You are to design the style sheet for this ticket, onto which each event can be entered as the programme becomes finalised. Some specific details which must occur are: the title of the festival, the year, and there must be space left for the event, location and seat number for those events where this is necessary, as well as price. Create a mock-up showing these details.

6   From the style sheet, design the **ticket** for a performance of *The Cherry Orchard* by Chekhov to be given between 1st and 9th of August in the Castle Court Theatre. Print out ten tickets and assign them numbers with the automatic page numbering facility in the desktop publishing package.

7 A travel agent has a stand at a Holiday Fair and requires a **folder** for the leaflets the public will take away. Prepare the design for this folder. Remember, this type of production would be passed on to a professional printer, as in-house printers are unlikely to cope with heavy-duty paper or card, as in this case. There would also be considerable finishing processes, like folding and gluing, to be done.

8 A boutique shop selling children's clothes requires a **label** for the neck part of each garment and a **swing ticket** to be attached to the sleeves. Although the shop trades as Youngsters, this need not be part of the label. An image is requested as part of these labels. The swing ticket lends itself to a non-rectangular shape, so try out some ideas to accommodate this.

APPENDICES

▼ Appendix One

Paper (Referred to as 'Stock')

In this course, you will probably output most of your documents to plain A4 paper, using either a laser or inkjet printer. However, a dramatic difference can be made to all your work by investing some time (and money) in the paper it is printed on.

Some decisions are made for you, because printers may have limitations with regard to the weight and surface of the paper you can use. Laser printers generally produce good results on weights between 80 and 120 gsm, making heavier paper and card unsuitable. Some colour inkjets produce very good results on ordinary copy paper, and excel on the specially treated paper for colour printouts. The greatest difference you can bring about in your output is to have the correct weight of paper, combined with the correct surface and a suitable colour.

Colour in paper is really about very subtle tints. Even a variation in the whiteness, together with a better quality, can make your output look professional. Consider, then, ranges in tints that reflect the subject of your document. For example, you may do a publication for a florist or gardener, when a tone towards green or earthy colours would strengthen your message. Paper which has a rippled or rough finish is not usually suitable for in-house printers.

The type of paper you will have used until now is probably bought in reams of 500 sheets and falls into the category of Bond paper. Dot matrix printers usually use continuous stationery. Once your publication is saved to disk for printing by a professional printer, the choice of paper types is wider and you should take advantage of this by taking time to select a paper that is ideal for your job and budget.

Calendered paper is manufactured as either coated or uncoated. Antique paper is used for books and has a rougher surface than calendered, which is smooth and used for magazines. You will also need to use paper which is opaque if you intend to have printed material on both sides. You should have samples to choose from for whichever job you are carrying out, as the paper is part of the message.

Conservation

Far from reducing the use of paper, computing has vastly increased its use and some measures should be undertaken by all users to conserve paper whenever possible. You are recommended to buy very small quantities of paper on which to try out your printer before buying in quantity, as it can be a very costly outlay.

Today we should consider recycled paper, which also comes in a wide variety of weights, colours and finishes for any jobs, although prices are as high as for standard types because recycling is a costly process. To conserve expensive paper, rough drafts should be printed on paper of a lighter weight, and at a lower resolution (180 dpi), to conserve toner or ink cartridges. Sometimes work schedules within a class or business can be structured to reuse pages which have very little print matter on them. Refillable cartridges should also be used wherever possible.

▼ Appendix Two
Paper Sizes

The size of paper which the printer can handle determines the majority of the output of an in-house desktop publisher. All printers will print on A4 and some on A3. However, the in-house publisher can use a professional printer to deal with any material which has special requirements in terms of paper size and quality, colour, volume and what are called finishing processes, like binding, folding and gluing. The desktop publisher will provide the printer with the drafts that have been produced and the disk containing the completed documents. With some communication between them, the computer user and the printer can come to an accurate understanding of what is required.

Below, you will see what each paper size is in relation to other sizes. The 'A' series measurement system is based on the '0' size, which is one square metre in area. Each size is exactly half the area of the size before it and is geometrically the same.

Name	Millimetres	Inches
A3	297 x 420	11.7 x 16.5
A4	210 x 297	8.3 x 11.7
A5	148 x 210	5.8 x 8.3
A6	105 x 148	4.1 x 5.8

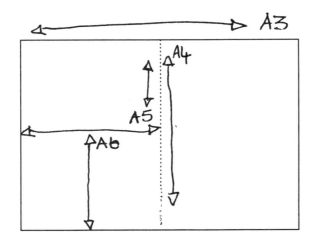

This diagram shows the most common paper sizes used in desktop publishing.

▼ APPENDIX THREE
FONT SAMPLES

The font samples included here are those that were used in the course more than once. They are set out so that you can compare one with another and select fonts as near as possible if you do not have the same ones in your application. These samples can also be used to examine more closely those features of typography that are covered in the introduction to this book.

You will see how distinct the two main typefaces are — the serif group first and then the cleaner, open style of the sans serif. You should try to use only a few typefaces in each publication and remember that it is easier on the reader to mix serif with serif and reserve the sans serif for subheadings or headlines. Notice, also, that all the fonts here were prepared in the same size (20 pts) but appear very different in size from each other. It is the width of the strokes that make up each character in that font that determines the overall size, as well as just how much space is provided either side of it.

The display fonts are shown separately, where you can see how some typefaces are only available in capitals (for example, Desdemona) and how difficult it would be to read text of any length in these faces — they are reserved for headlines.

Wingdings appears last, showing the symbols that can be obtained for each character of the keyboard.

ABCDEFGHIJKLMNOPQRSTUVWXYZ
abcdefghijklmnopqrstuvwxyz

Times New Roman

ABCDEFGHIJKLMNOPQRSTUVWXYZ
abcdefghijklmnopqrstuvwxyz

Palatino

ABCDEFGHIJKLMNOPQRSTUVWXYZ
abcdefghijklmnopqrstuvwxyz

Bright

ABCDEFGHIJKLMNOPQRSTUVWXYZ
abcdefghijklmnopqrstuvwxyz

Minister Book

ABCDEFGHIJKLMNOPQ
RSTUVWXYZ
abcdefghijklmnopqrstuvwxyz

Concerto
(Concerto)

ABCDEFGHIJKLMNOPQRSTUVWXYZ
abcdefghijklmnopqrstuvwxyz

Cambridge

ABCDEFGHIJKLMNOPQRSTUVWXYZ
abcdefghijklmnopqrstuvwxyz

Brush
Script

𝕬𝕭𝕮𝕯𝕰𝕱𝕲𝕳𝕴𝕵𝕶𝕷𝕸𝕹𝕺𝕻𝕼𝕽𝕾𝕿𝖀𝖁𝖂𝖃𝖄𝖅
abcdefghijklmnopqrstuvwxyz

TUDOR
(Tudor)

ABCDEFGHIJKLMNOPQRSTUVWXYZ
abcdefghijklmnopqrstuvwxyz

Bodoni
Book

ABCDEFGHIJKLMNOPQRSTUVWXYZ
abcdefghijklmnopqrstuvwxyz

Helvetica

ABCDEFGHIJKLMNOPQRSTUVWXYZ
abcdefghijklmnopqrstuvwxyz

**Arial
Rounded MT**

ABCDEFGHIJKLMNOPQRSTUVWXYZ
abcdefghijklmnopqrstuvwxyz

AvantGarde

ABCDEFGHIJKLMNOPQRSTUVWXYZ
abcdefghijklmnopqrstuvwxyz

Ravel

ABCDEFGHIJKLMNOPQRSTUVWXYZ
abcdefghijklmnopqrstuvwxyz **Drury Lane**

ABCDEFGHIJKLMNOPQRSTUVWXYZ
ABCDEFGHIJKLMNOPQRSTUVWXYZ DESDEMONA

ABCDEFGHIJKLMNOPQRSTUVWXYZ
abcdefghijklmnopqrstuvwxyz *Sage*

THE COMPLETE WINGDING FONT

✌👌👍👎☜☞☝✋☺☻☹💣☀☠⚐⚑✈☼♨❄

ABCDE F GH I J K L M NO P Q R S T

✝✝✠✠✡☪

UVWXYZ

a b c d e f g h i j k l m n o p q r

♋♌♍♎♏♐♑♒♓⚹&●○■□□□□

s t u v w x y z ; . , '

◆◆◆❖◆☒☒⌘▭✉✉🕯

1 2 3 4 5 6 7 8 9 0 - =

📁📄📄📄⌛⌨🖱💿📷📪💾

! " £ $ % ^ & * ( ) _ +

✏✂⚫🔔♈📖✉☎☾♉📧

@ : ? ✂

🖱💻✍⊙💾

▼ APPENDIX FOUR
PRINTING

Satisfying the client brief on screen is usually easy, once the desktop publishing package has been mastered. Any difficulties that desktop publishers encounter usually occur at print time. Below are some guidelines which, over the years, both as an individual desktop publisher and as a teacher, I have found make for a smoother sequence from idea to hard copy.

1   Make sure the correct driver for your printer is installed on your computer.

2   If **more than one printer** is installed, ensure that the one you are targeting is indicated as the target printer in the print dialog box.

3   Make sure the **leads** between computer and printer are correctly connected and that both pieces of hardware are switched on!

4   If your document is designed on screen with a **landscape** orientation, be sure that the Wide option is chosen in the print dialog box.

5   If your printer requires **paper to be aerated** before it will receive it, make sure you do so (to avoid paper jams).

6   Ensure that you use only the weights and types of paper recommended. Remember, too, that some **preprinted stationery** is not suited to laser printing, as the inks can smudge when it passes through the in-house printer.

7   If you are working under **Windows**, close the print manager to cancel print jobs if you have a problem with a document. This clears the memory of both computer and printer, to start fresh again when you send data next time.

8   Some packages enable you to **Shrink to Fit** or choose a percentage scale at printing. This is a most useful feature when an element in a document is just oversized or reaches the extremities of the margins and would be helped by more white space.

9   Work from the **C drive** for most printing jobs, as it is quicker.

10 Choose the option to **Grey Out** images when printing, as this speeds up the return to screen, and have documents on screen at 50% to see the overall look when you wish to identify layout problems from the rough draft.

11 Check that the paper is being fed into the printer so that its horizontal position is correct. Many documents appear to have unequal margins when it is only the position of the paper that is causing the problem. (That is one value of the **Print Test** at startup, besides indicating the toner condition and whether the heads in inkjet printers need cleaning.)

12 Print only the **number of pages required** each time, not the whole document, by choosing Range and the page or pages necessary.

13   Spend some time examining your **print dialog box**. The information on this is stored with the file and should be checked each time you recall a document, as your intention this time may be different and you may not want 10 copies as for the previous time!

14   Although it is recommended that we conserve paper, it is usually unwise to reuse paper in inkjet and laser printers as this is a prime cause of paper jams. However, some stock should be allowed for experimenting with ideas for documents, when a new printer is installed and also for important jobs nearing their deadline. Your printer is the most significant piece of equipment besides the computer, and the direct communicator with your public, so it is worth getting to know it well. Every printer has its own unique set of features which can be used to your advantage.

▼ APPENDIX FIVE
PROOF CORRECTION MARKS

	Mark in text	Mark in margin or notes
No new paragraph		
Delete		or
Insert inverted commas		
Centre		
Change to capital		
Start new paragraph		
Reduce space between words		or
Embolden		
Change order of words or characters		often with numbers or trs
Insert comma	or	
Insert a space		
Insert a full stop		
Indent given width (characters or mm)		
Insert apostrophe		
Change capital to lower case		
Close up		
Lower case (small character)		l.c.
Upper case (capital)		u.c.

▼ APPENDIX SIX

TEXT FOR WORD PROCESSING AND CONVERTING TO ASCII

N.B. These texts are available on the Student Disk

ARCHITEC.TXT (FOR USE WITH EXERCISES 42 AND 43)

The restoration of the Saloon and stairhall of Number 85 was commenced in January 1992. Throughout 1992 and 1993 thorough research and conservation was carried out in order to return these interiors to their early eighteenth-century appearance. The plaster work was carefully cleaned and the original colour scheme has now been reinstated.

Two of the many features of this superb Georgian house are the Saloon and grand stairhall.

Particularly noteworthy is the lavishly decorated plaster work of the Saloon, initially created by the Swiss stuccodore Paolo and Filippo Lafranchini. The project has rekindled the spirit of Georgian craftsmanship and is recognised as a unique achievement of architectural and historical importance. Gallaher (Dublin) Limited is proud to have been involved as patron in preserving this vital part of our national heritage.

Number 85 St Stephen's Green is attributed to Richard Castle,* Ireland's leading Palladian designer of the mid-eighteenth century. The grandest and most consciously architectural interior in Newman House is the Saloon on the first floor of Number 85 St Stephen's Green. Especially noteworthy is the room's coved ceiling which is decorated with a figurative plaster work scheme. The Apollo room is a diminutive interior with stucco decoration by the Lafranchini brothers. The decorative scheme depicts Apollo, god of arts, surrounded by the nine muses of the arts.

*See History of a Famous Residence, p 90, 1930 edition

(227 words)

EXAMP.TXT (FOR USE WITH EXERCISE 33)

From January on, students and teachers make constant references to Examinations. Long before that, examination bodies have set the papers as a result of meetings that had taken place early last year, and even before that someone somewhere decided to make changes or introduce a new examination or set out the papers differently.

Students are relaxed in September when they join a course after the long break and the thoughts of tests and study are far away. It may not be until the first essays are due to be handed up that the reality strikes and genuine work has to be started. The academic year is very short with some years having an exceptionally short last term which is virtually packed with examinations. Many applicants for exams do not work early

enough to give themselves the best chance to be in control of the situation. Instead they waste the early months and approach the exams with a poor grasp of practical and theoretical ability.

Not so the students of the Desktop Publishing Course. Many of them have produced work of an exceptionally high standard since November and from January on are perfecting their techniques so that as soon as they see the paper they know exactly what to do. Some even prepare sketches so that they can work from their own visuals once they have understood the requirements of the examination paper.

Examinations which need a lot of reading as preparation are often the ones students could do the most to improve in if they adopted a technique now recognised as a major factor in success in written exams - that is to spend short spells of time with frequent reference to the same texts as a learning aid. Frequency and recency it is called in the business.

Teachers are afraid that if the student body did learn like that, some deep facts would be overlooked, but this method does provide pegs for students to hang other facts on. Many degrees and diplomas have been achieved by this method and it is felt that Second and Third level students would benefit by trying it too. There is expected to be a recommendation going out in the media very soon to catch those students who face the summer again this year with examinations on their minds. Notebooks and prompt lists are also a great help, but nothing helps one learn as much as careful and regular reading, whatever the subject.

Writers of text books have made great efforts lately to provide excellent illustrations and clear paragraph headings for new topics to aid the learning process. Moves like this have helped so many students, as well as careful note taking from these books.

(450 words)

HOUSE.TXT (FOR USE WITH EXERCISE 47)

This development is being undertaken by the country's most experienced architect and builders working as a team from the initial stages of planning to the completion of the property.

The original site has been secured many years ago but left in the hands of the occupants until the demise of the leaseholder. During that time several overall plans had been devised and worked on in outline only. Eventually, taking into account the developments in the surrounding areas, one of these early plans was chosen. Builder and Architect applied the most advanced techniques to every aspect of this huge undertaking, from enclosing the site from the adjoining properties to its promotion on completion. There are three types of property on this undulating site, each development given unique views and approaches to the countryside and infrastructure. Entering the Coopers Yard the three-storey houses can only be described as modern but adhering to the traditional qualities of family and community living. There are facilities for car parking, garaging, storage and field games without having all on view. Carefully designed areas of foliage and grass give openness and freedom to those who wish to have access to the countryside. Inside, the three-bedroom property has the expected standards of finish to all kitchen, bathroom and ensuite fitments, being designed by Hall and Harris especially for this development.

Two-storey terraced houses form an unusual feature of this area, with just 52 units divided between the four sites. These are mainly two-bedroom houses with eight three-bedroom styles in the area near the apartment block. Apartments like these rarely come on the market. They have all been developed from a widely accepted formula that has sold well for the last four years, but given individuality by being personalised for this site. This means that, wherever possible, the living room has been placed to give the best view or the best light as a priority and the other rooms designed to lead from this, while bedrooms are accessed from another direction. There are landscape features to the apartments but in keeping with the open aspect of the site as a whole. The properties in all three categories are Gas Fired Centrally Heated and open fireplaces are a standard in all living rooms.

Interior decor has been designed by Phillip Ketchly and Company and your individual needs can be met in consultation with one of his representatives.

(397 words)

HCI.TXT (FOR USE WITH EXERCISES 34 AND 38)

Within the next eight to ten years I expect there to be many developments in the field of human - computer interaction. I think one of the most important will be standardisation at the interface both in input by the user and in response by the computer.

I envisage much less keyboard use for strings of commands at input and an immediate move to the benefits of updated operating software which will offer a great improvement in the tone and range of its response. This update identifies the type of error made and has a less aggressive 'tone' in communicating with the user.

With regard to the keyboard itself, I feel a move will have to be made before too long to get acceptance of a more suitable layout and possibly a design which includes a trackball or similar input device as a part of its surface. Steps like these would change the image of the computer from being 'shut off' and only available for specialist use, to its acceptance as a 'natural' part of business, functional and family life.

Even in homes it is housed in an office-like environment and when in a living or family room it is thought to be out of place. [I feel, however, that the arrival of Minitel will shortly change this for us here as it has done for the French.]

I hope we can look forward to quick and easy access to computers with maybe varying levels of interaction once the 'novice' period has been passed. One major contribution to this objective would be an emphasis in hardware design for integration into ordinary family life: and we can point to telephone design as moving rapidly recently to fuller integration into decor of many types.

Another form of standardisation that is shortly to be expected is the high resolution screen with, of course, colour monitors. I feel the demand for Windows will account for the rapid move to high specification VDUs and I think Windows will provide the impetus for manufacturers to develop software for a much wider range of uses than we see at present. Many children will be users much earlier than we have at present and using computers as a standard part of their homework and research for projects which is so much a part of a student's curriculum now.

I see human - computer interaction providing a very wide range of interaction to services like Viewdata via educational resources like libraries, simply because of the developments in telecommunications together with easier and attractive means of interaction with virtually error-free routing to the user's goals. This would mean that the on-line help would have to be immediately available and executable just as easily, if it was necessary at all. If computers could interpret the user's needs when an input error was made this whole area of side-tracking for help could be avoided.

Eventually I see computers becoming an extension of our natural environment and being extraordinarily sensitive.

So far we use our eyes and fingers with keyboard and mouse for interaction, but developments in the immediate future are likely to bring the full body into action with gesture, tracing of eye movements and changes in stance and head position being used as interactors. In the future we will seem to have been very primitive. Virtual Reality is the environment for exploring the opportunities that total bodily involvement could create, both as a working tool as at present in flight and space travel preparation and as a research tool to find out more about human behaviour. There is of course an expectation that Virtual Reality will provide a wide range of entertainment environments too.

Early in the history of the development of computers, Hypertext and Powerbook were predicted by their developers to be of immense use. It seems that, after all, this is just where human - computer interaction is going now. Human - computer interaction will enable computers to become a very personalised tool, enabling computers to recognise a wider and finer range of the user's behaviour - and hopefully be able to 'tune' its responses, as if trained, to the current session of interaction by reference to earlier sessions. I feel the linear use of computers which we have today will change to a tangential and cross-referenced form of interaction which in itself can be mapped by the system to leave human beings to be more creative and less dependent on the spade work of life and leisure. [I wonder how the present Expert Systems with their inference engines will be seen in the light of developments in the fields I have just mentioned.]

At present the computer system and software developers dictate what is available to us - perhaps developments will enable a personal or family computer resource to interact with other systems just when the individual is ready to do so - in other words keep pace with individual developments of personality and intellect and interest, opening up wider vistas, as travel and television have for us up to now.

No survey of future developments in human - computer interaction should end without wide ranging consideration of the computer interaction sought by the disabled. Already the breath, eyeblinks and chin movements are interfaced in education and on life-support levels. The inferencing interface mentioned above may be able to interpret unsteady users' movements, or a particular movement of trunk or limbs to good effect to influence their living and educational environment. I would hope that speech and language learning for reading and communication skills for deaf and speech-impaired users would be available so that the present laborious character, word and phrase building may be overtaken by software that creates clauses and sentences of a non-standard type for true conversation.

I feel great strides will be made in developing software for the areas touched on in this report, simply because human - computer interaction will become a more exact science aided by its own computers and be seen very soon as a worthy area for investment of money and time by developers.

(1,006 words)

MUSEUM.TXT (FOR USE WITH EXERCISE 49)

The early Christian period was very influential: designers looked at the church plate and jewellery which survived from that period. A large number of ancient architectural remains from across Europe were also studied. Most importantly they studied ancient manuscripts for information about French civilisation and history.

Another vital asset was that a common language was still intact. They found that the French people were inspired by songs and telling stories and the cultures of many European people were also drawn upon. 'People who had been told for years that these were savages with a barbarous language and no evidence of civilisation were persuaded that it was not so.'

One feature of Irish distinction was for the Irish language to be used beside English and in the ancient Gaelic script. This was one of the few scripts that varied from the Roman and Italic. Ireland had a unique opportunity to develop its own typographic style. Visually pleasing rounded letter forms were seen on almost everything, from government forms and postage stamps to street and place names. Type founders and designers had kept faithfully to this way of printing, but in the 1960s the Minister of Education said that all schoolchildren should learn Irish in the 'Modern' Roman type. This caused some people to become quite angry that the Irish script was no longer to have as wide a use. A proponent of the former, Canon Ulick J Bourke, wrote in 1856 that 'Greece has never really suffered the disgrace of having her national language thus paraded in alien costume - Ireland has. Her written language has been tortured into a thousand ignoble shapes, which have made it appear to the eyes of some as the pencilled jargon of slaves.' Others would argue that Roman type would always be more readable than Irish type and it would have been easier to make the Roman hot metal type (which had become nearly extinct by the 1960s).

The new opportunities available with the growing technologies have also accommodated some Irish typefaces.

(338 words)

NEWMAN.TXT (FOR USE WITH EXERCISE 37)

The preservation of Ireland's architectural heritage is widely accepted as a task of vital importance for the 1990s. Gallaher (Dublin) Limited has acknowledged the importance of this by giving its support to one of the country's leading conservation enterprises - the restoration of Newman House.

The objectives of the project were threefold: to preserve for prosperity a unique and very beautiful building; to encourage excellence in contemporary Irish craftsmanship; and to bring to life again its architectural excellence.

Numbers 85 and 86 St Stephen's Green are two of the best and most original Georgian townhouses in Dublin. By good fortune these important buildings were united in common ownership in the mid-nineteenth century when acquired by the Catholic University of Ireland, the precursor of modern University College Dublin. The property was later named Newman House in honour of the University's first rector John Henry, Cardinal Newman. In 1755 Number 85 was purchased by Richard Chapel Whaley who also acquired the adjoining site and, in 1765, began building 86 St Stephen's Green. A rare wax portrait depicts Whaley with his young wife Anne Ward and their seven children. 'Buck' Whaley, the notorious rake and gambler, was the couple's second son. In the wax portrait he is depicted kneeling and holding a rattle to the right of the central group.

In November of 1851 John Henry Newman was formally invited to become rector of the new Catholic University of Ireland. In the following year Newman delivered a series of lectures on the scope and nature of university education - the renowned discourses later published as 'The Idea of a University'.

In one of his most famous passages Newman held forth a challenge and a prophecy for Ireland and for his university. James Joyce was a student of Philosophy and English at University College from 1899 to 1902. The old Physics Theatre of the University is located on the first floor of Number 85; it was in this room that Joyce gave his maiden speech to the Literary and Historical Society.

Joyce later used the Physics Theatre as a setting for an encounter in 'A Portrait of the Artist as a Young Man'. In 1854 the newly established Catholic University of Ireland received its first students in Number 86 St Stephen's Green.

Since this time the house has seen successive generations of students. The worn threshold of Number 86 is an evocative image for many graduates with fond memories of the building.

In 1884 the English poet and Jesuit priest, Gerard Manley Hopkins, was appointed Professor of Classics at University College. While in Dublin Hopkins wrote the sequence of poems now known as 'The Terrible Sonnets'. These six poems are a vivid expression of Hopkins' loneliness and despair. While intensely personal, they powerfully evoke the desolation and spiritual turmoil of human existence. Hopkins died at Newman House on 8th June 1889. His study in Number 86 is now open to the public. The original home of University College Dublin is a building that has close associations with such original thinkers as John Henry, Cardinal Newman, the poet Gerard Manley Hopkins and latterly with James Joyce and Flann O'Brien.

Gallaher also believes in the power of original thinking and are proud to have been involved as patrons in preserving this vital part of our heritage; a fine example of how the past can enrich present-day life and enhance the lives of future generations.

(566 words)

TECHNO.TXT (FOR USE WITH EXERCISES 20, 21, 22, 35, 38 AND 41)

Anyone entering an administrative environment should be fully conversant with what is called Office Technology. Each component of this matrix has an individual part to play in communications as well as being a vital link in the chain of faster more efficient data exchange.

We can see from the widespread use of Word Processing that computerisation has become the essential tool for administrative information gathering, output, and recording. The integrated office system has been with us now for long enough for what used to be the slow interaction between one software package and another to take place on screen and almost simultaneously. Data can be captured, stored, retrieved and reused in an entirely different package within seconds and by the same user. End users are increasingly imaginative with the use of the integrated package and develop personal routes and shortcuts to the desired objective.

The stand-alone PC was eagerly accepted by many and abhorred by just as many employees. Just around the corner was the Network! This has called for a new attitude to work practices and what can be described as ownership of a project or part of it. Users may indeed be responsible for a particular part of, say, the design of a building, but interaction with others doing their part may be very limited, and involvement in the finished product when bringing it all together may not take place. Job satisfaction comes from other areas than the finished design.

The network has placed the responsibility for the technical integrity of the system in the hands of an expert who may or may not work in a hands-on role on the project. Some users are much happier knowing that specialist help is on hand when problems to do with the system occur; however, some would like to deal with a network manager who understands the needs of users and the priorities they have in their work load.

Telecommunications advancements have impinged on all administrative staff. Not only have we seen an exceptional explosion in Telesales recently but there is an expectation that all employees will be conversant with Databases provided by the country's Television and Telecommunications service. So many companies rely on up to the minute information on currencies, credit ratings, sales figures, trends in markets, movement of goods and money that employees are expected to be able to retrieve this data from whatever source the company is linked to.

Some businesses stand or fall just on the strengths of their computerised systems and their network capabilities, the travel industry for instance.

In this case we cannot imagine a successful venture unless mobile phones, fax machines, photocopiers, modems and computers work in tandem to provide the

proprietor and their clients with communications facilities of the highest order.

Networks and telecommunications have brought widely spread organisations together in a way that ignores time and space differences. Local networks linked to others and linked via bridges to wider networks means that data captured in one location can be available in another part of the world and acted upon within minutes.

The social implications of these recent changes are wide indeed. As users and employees we can be forgiven at times if we are wary of interaction with people we are not face to face with. We may not be interacting with another person on the phone when voice recognition becomes more widely available. We may be booking our tickets for theatres and trains with pre-recorded voices which can interpret our requests and send out our order immediately. We may work more closely with people on other networks than with the people in the same building. This raises questions about the value we place on human interaction and increased preciousness of face to face communication and personal relationships. Schools and parents should be aware of how different the world young people will be working in is from the one they went into and what limited chances there are in some employment for people to be themselves.

(665 words)

▼ APPENDIX SEVEN

IMAGES FOR SCANNING PRACTICE

N.B. These images are available on the Student Disk

Many teachers will have libraries of their own to draw on to provide suitable images for the exercises in this course. For those who have not, the following pages have the images laid out in such a way as to enable students or teachers to scan them. Each image can not only be used for the exercises as indicated but, of course, can be cropped, reshaped or adapted to other documents.

Most of them can be copied by students in a basic paint program and saved for importation to the desktop publishing application. Used as an elementary reference these illustrations can form the basis of many lessons to encourage students' creativity and widen their use of software and peripherals.

It would be wise to copy the images from the student disk that accompanies this book into a directory on the hard drive for speedier importation. This procedure follows the recommendations in Good Work Practices (page 12) and should also be adopted for scanned work undertaken as well as in preparation for using the text in Appendix Six.

*Images used in Part 1
Exercises 1-20 and
appearing on the
accompanying disk*

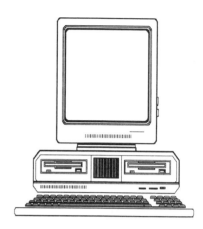

Images used in Part 2

Milettes

Marvellous

Meals

**25 Stockton Mall
Open 9am - 11pm
Phone 4354771**

*Images used in
Part 2 continued*

Images used in Part 4

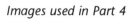

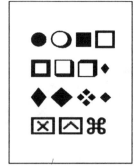

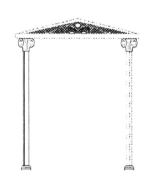

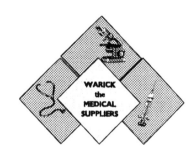

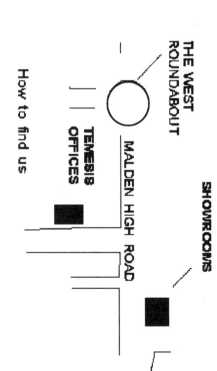

How to find us

THE WEST
ROUNDABOUT

TEMESIS
OFFICES

MALDEN HIGH ROAD

SHOWROOMS

WARICK
the
MEDICAL
SUPPLIERS

*Images used in
Part 4 continued*

ISBN 1-85471-600-X

9 781854 716002

Some ideas to use or develop for your own documents

▼ APPENDIX EIGHT
GLOSSARY

Alignment, horizontal
The placement of text, usually in paragraphs, on a horizontal plane.

Alignment, vertical
The placement of text, usually in paragraphs, on a vertical plane.

Ascender
The top part of lower-case letters which reach above the x-height (f, h, and k are examples).

ASCII (American Standard Code for Information Interchange)
A computer code for text, which is compatible across all applications.

Aspect ratio
The proportion of height to width in an image. 1:1 is the original proportion; any other ratio represents a distortion.

Baseline
An unseen line on which characters rest and from which the x-height and leading is measured.

Baseline shift
Characters rest on an imaginary line from which their size is determined. There are times when it is necessary to move a character up or down (bullets, for example) from this imaginary line, and this is described as a baseline shift.

Bullet
A symbol used to organise text. It starts a paragraph and is an aid to reading and understanding.

CD-ROM (Compact Disk)
A storage medium of huge capacity. Software is now available for installing programs, receiving add-ons and extra fonts, as well as providing libraries of illustrations and images on CD-ROMs.

Callout
An insert in newspapers and magazines, placed across columns, with an extract from the text in a larger point size, often with graphic lines to add emphasis.

Caption
Information, in a small font, about an illustration, photograph, or diagram, placed originally above (hence *cap*tion) but now mostly placed below these elements.

Case
Describes a character in terms of capital (upper) or small appearance (lower), derived from their respective position in printers' cases where the typefaces were kept.

Clip art
Illustrative material bought from software providers, either free from copyright restraints or with minimal charge, for use in desktop publishing. Clip art originated on disk but is now widely available on CD-ROM.

Colour separations
These are separate printouts for each colour used in a document. Thus, if a page uses two colours besides black, three printouts will be needed, to show which part of the whole requires which colour ink. The printer uses these printouts to make printing plates for each ink.

Copy and paste
A routine to store an element (temporarily) in memory and duplicate it in another location; this does not alter the original in any way. (*see also* multiple paste)

Correction marks
These are marks widely used and understood in the printing and publishing world to indicate corrections in draft text from proofreader to printer or desktop publisher.

CPI
Characters per inch, horizontally.

Crop marks
These are marks indicating where the exact limit of the page is. They are used when the

area of the document is smaller than the paper size and show exactly where the paper will be trimmed.

Cropping

This technique is used to take away a portion of an image and leave the required part for further transformation as necessary.

Custom columns

These are measurements of column width put in by the desktop publisher which are not standard within the application.

Defaults

Measurements, instructions and decisions which the application will resort to if the user does not override them.

Delete

To remove (a marked or highlighted) element, with no facility to replace it.

Descender

That part of a lower-case character which reaches below the baseline (g, j, p and y are examples).

Display text or fonts

These are fonts which are unsuitable for continuous text but are ideal for headlines or short eye-catching sections of information.

DPI (dots per square inch)

Screen resolution and print resolution are described in terms of dpi. The higher the number, the better. Low resolution printing (180 or less) is used for faster draft output.

Drafts

These are hard copies of publications which are in the process of revision. There are often several drafts before a document is ready for volume production.

Drop capitals

This term describes the use of initial capitals which are much larger than the rest of the line and therefore reach down into the paragraph.

Edit

To alter, in any way, either text or images.

em

A unit of measurement which is the square of the indent or width of the character **m**.

en

Half an em.

EPS (Encapsulated PostScript format)

This is a file format where a graphic or document is written in the PostScript language. Preparing material in this format enables it to be printed, as all the codes are contained in the description.

Exporting text

This procedure is used to store text as a file (in ASCII), which originated within the desktop publishing application. The text becomes an element in its own right for use in other situations.

Fill

This term describes the facility to fill in geometric shapes with a gradient of shades from 10% to 100% of either a colour (then called a tint) or grey to black.

Font

A font is a family of typefaces all with the same basic characteristics. As an example, Palatino is not only a serifed typeface but can be adapted to be emboldened, italicised and condensed. The characteristics are applied to every letter, punctuation mark, symbol and figure, when describing a font.

Footer

This is brief text material which occurs within the bottom margin and repeats on subsequent pages. Often set up on a style sheet.

Footnote

A footnote appears at the bottom of the page of text to which it refers. Its presence is indicated by a symbol (usually an asterisk) in the text, and again just before the footnote. It is usually set in small type.

Gatefold brochure

Landscape A4 is folded twice into three equal portions. The last panel is placed inside the first fold.

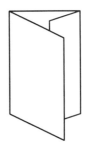

Grids

These are used to determine the layout of a publication and to ensure that double-page spreads are unified. They aid in the placement of the various elements of a document, because text and images can be set to them. A Snap to Guides feature ensures that elements are attracted to them.

Graphic

This describes the drawing features of a desktop publishing application (the line, ellipse and rectangle, for example). Can also refer to an illustration, either line art or artwork.

Greeking

Showing text either on screen or in sketches in an unreadable form because it is too small to be read. Indicating only the areas taken up by text in small point size.

Gutters

The space between columns.

Header

This is brief text material which is placed in the top margin. It is often repeated on each page and therefore should be set up on the style sheet.

Hard copy

The printed output from any computer program.

I-beam

This is the shape the pointer or cursor changes to when working in text mode.

Image control

This is a facility to change the contrast and brightness of an image. It can be done either as part of the scanning process or within the desktop publishing application.

Indent

This is a feature of paragraph starts where the first word begins usually 3 mm in from the left margin. Its function is to identify for the reader new paragraphs and so aid reading.

Kerning

This technique is used to regularise the spacing between particular pairs of letters, and especially in larger point sizes. Kerning can be used to expand the space (in the case of il and especially in larger point sizes. Kerning can be used to expand the space (in the case of il and it for example) or to draw certain pairs together, as in aw, yo.

Landscape

This is a page layout where the page width is greater than the depth.

Leading

The space between lines of type, taking descenders, ascenders and an extra proportion of white space (so that these do not meet) into account. Leading is standard at approximately one fifth more than the point size.

Linking

This is a facility many desktop publishing programs offer to join one file with others to form a larger document at print time, to aid pagination and layout decisions. It is easier to handle small files and then build them into larger ones.

Lower case

A lower-case letter is one not in capitals (i.e. small letters).

Margins

The space from the edge of the page to the area designated to contain the document is the margin. It appears on all sides of the page and is often set wider at the inside to accommodate binding.

Multiple paste

After copying an item within a document, some applications enable the user to state how many copies are required and at what distance from each other they should be displayed.

Object linking and embedding

The facility for bringing images, text and sections of databases and spreadsheets from the package they were created in directly into the document being worked on.

OCR (Optical Character Recognition)

This is a data capture method where text is digitised by a scanner for computer output.

Opaque

This is a description of the characteristics of paper which is thick enough to prevent light showing through.

Orientation

This term describes the page layout. It is either portrait (tall) or landscape (wide).

Orphans

When the first line of a paragraph is at the foot of a page or column. It should either be joined with the rest of the paragraph or made into more than one line. (*see also* widow)

Page numbering or pagination

Pages can be numbered automatically if the style sheet has been set up to indicate the number's exact position on the pages of the document. The pages need not start at 1.

Pitch

A horizontal measurement of characters per inch.

Pixel editing

All displays on screen are made up of pixels (the smallest unit of a screen display — a *pic*ture *el*ement). By moving in on the screen very closely (at least 200%), you can identify each pixel that makes up an item. Images can be edited by adding or removing pixels.

Point

The unit used to measure the height of a character. One point is one seventy-second of an inch, therefore text of 72 points is one inch high.

Preferences

Computer applications are installed with defaults set, but users can override these through preference settings to customise the program.

Process colour

In this process, colours are used in images and illustrations in fine and smooth gradients, more like photography.

Proof correction marks *see* correction marks

Proportional spacing

This type of spacing produces text which provides the same space for each character, regardless of its width. Courier is an example of a proportionally spaced typeface.

`This is proportional spacing.`

Register Marks

This is a symbol placed on camera-ready material to ensure accurate positioning during photography.

Reversed text

Text is normally black on a white ground. However, for effect and emphasis, the desktop publisher can create an area of grey to black on which a white or 'reversed' text is placed.

Rotated text

Most desktop publishing programs enable text and images to be rotated; that is, set at an angle to the horizontal.

Scanning

This is a technique for transferring images, or text (via Optical Character Recognition software), into digitised form. A laser beam 'reads' the data and transfers it to the computer program, from where it can be edited and stored as an ordinary file.

Signature

Printed folded sheets ready to be sewn, with others, into a book. Each signature usually consists of 16 pages.

Snap (to guides)

The snap feature is either on or off. If it is on, its function is to make elements of a document jump to the guides and so ensure accurate placement.

Spell checker

A spell checker is an essential part of a word processing or desktop publishing program and it should be used to check for typographical errors and genuine spelling errors. However, it does not find all errors, like plurals and synonyms, so you must rely upon close proofreading to be sure of an error-free document.

Spot colour

Using colour in this way is simple and inexpensive. An area of text, a graphic feature or an image is designated to be printed in a single shade or colour. If you were to mix the cyan, magenta, yellow and black components to make a particular shade, this would remain constant throughout its application in solid lines and fills.

Standoff

The distance between a frame and the surrounding text.

Stock

Paper is referred to as stock when purchased in large quantities.

Style sheet

The terms 'master' or 'template' are used to mean the same as style sheet. These are page description files which set out the page measurements and repeating features like margins, headers, footers, graphic details and page numbering, as well as typestyle specifications.

Tabs or tabular stops

These are preset or user-defined points along the text line, at which columns of figures or information is to start. The tab key is used to reach these points.

Text wrap

Text wrap options are used to determine the way frames containing images or text are abutted by the main text of the document. The main text can flow around the frame (on three sides only) or jump the entire horizontal area occupied by the frame, as well as closely follow the outline of an image.

Thesaurus

Many text-managing programs provide a thesaurus facility which enables the user to seek meanings for words and alternatives to avoid repetitive use of the same phrase or word.

TIFF (Tagged-image file format)

A standard graphics file format.

Tile

To tile is to request the printout of an A3 page, for example, to be produced on an A4 printer, by splitting up the page into sections which overlap slightly and so provide a reasonable idea of what the finished product would be like if handled by a professional printing house.

Tracking

The space set by the program between each letter and letter combination. This measurement can be altered to be 'tight', 'loose' or 'very loose' in most applications.

Transformation

This term is used to describe the changes imposed, usually on an image, during preparation for a publication. Several transformations could be undertaken — such as rotate, shadow, image control, cropping and copying — on each image.

Typeface

A typeface describes the characters, symbols, punctuation marks, widths, size and general appearance of a particular design of text. An example would be Times New Roman, 18 pts, italic.

Typographers' quotes

A facility in Preferences to provide quotes that form professional double and single inverted commas.

Upper case

Capital letters.

Widow

This is an undesirable feature, where the last line of a paragraph appears at the top of the next page or column in a document. (*see also* orphan)

WIMPS

Stands for Window, Icon, Menu, Pointer and Selection, which are characteristics of the Windows environment.

Wingdings

This is a typeface, therefore text, which is made up entirely of symbols. These can be used like text, but appear as images. (*see* Appendix Seven)

WYSIWYG

(Pronounced wisywig) What you see is what you get. Applications are described as providing this feature when the screen image is exactly like the finished product.

x-height

This term describes the measurement of the height of the lower-case letters within a typeface which have no ascenders or descenders (a, e, c, r, m, o and, of course, x, are examples).

Zoom

To zoom in or out is to cause the screen to produce a close-up or distant view of the text or object under scrutiny.